Australia's Greatest PEOPLE & THEIR Achievements

LINSAY KNIGHT

RANDOM HOUSE AUSTRALIA

A Random House book
Published by Random House Australia Pty Ltd
Level 3, 100 Pacific Highway, North Sydney NSW 2060
www.randomhouse.com.au

First published by Random House Australia in 2013

WARNING: Aboriginal readers, please be advised that images of
Aboriginal people who might be deceased appear in this book.

Addresses for companies within the Random House Group can be
found at www.randomhouse.com.au /offices

National Library of Australia Cataloguing-in-Publication entry
Author: Knight, Linsay, 1952–
Title: Australia's greatest people and their achievements
ISBN: 978 0 85798 020 5 (pbk)
Target Audience: For primary school age
Subjects: Celebrities – Australia – Biography – Juvenile literature
          Australia – Biography – Juvenile literature
Dewey Number: 994.0922

Cover image © Robert Churchill/Getty Images
Cover and internal design by Liz Seymour
Printed and bound in China by Everbest Printing Ltd

CONTENTS

Fitzroy
Crossing NORTHERN
Fitzroy Tennant Creek
Grange
GREAT SANDY MACDONNELL
ble Bar DESERT Mt. Ziel Alice
4,955 Springs
L. Amadeus
RA LI

US DESERT Ayers Rock 2,845
BSON Ernabella
Oodnadatta
AUSTRALIA L. Eyre
Laverton GR. AUSTRALIA
VICTORIA DESERT SOUTH
bor Plain Torrens
Nullar Penong Woomera
Port Au
GREAT Pt. Pi
ALIAN BIGHT
Ade
Kan
garoo
Gamb

Introduction

Australia is a great country. Our land is rich in natural resources, we have a fair and democratic system of government, beautiful beaches, cities and outback landscapes. Most important of all, Australia is full of great people who have made and who continue to make it the lucky country it is today.

Being 'great' is quite different from being famous or being a celebrity. It is hard to define, yet just about everyone can agree that someone like Joan Sutherland or Don Bradman was a great person. Greatness is something to do with making a special, lasting contribution that everyone remembers and appreciates – and always will. So it's about achievements and success, but it's also about character, perseverance and uniqueness.

Greatness is often recognised by official awards such as the Order of Australia, various sporting medals and performing arts statuettes like the Logies. Many of these recipients are included in this book. Some of these awards are voted on by everyone. You probably have some strong views on who you think is great. If you believe we have left out someone who should have been here, why not start your own list?

The great people we have chosen have achieved their greatness in many different areas – science, sport, business, education, politics, exploration, entertainment, art literature, social justice – just about every different type of activity a human being can undertake.

Of course there are other people – the unsung heroes, the quiet achievers – whose greatness may be recognised by just a few people, or hardly anyone. And yet often they have been just as essential in making Australia a great place, so we salute them too.

This is a book about great Australians, but it is written for all Australians, especially those just setting out on life's journey, who will work together in the future to make sure that Australia keeps on being the really great country we know and love.

LINSAY KNIGHT

"Ambition leads me not only farther than any other man has been before me, but as far as I think it possible for man to go."

– *Captain James Cook*

PIONEERING AUSTRALIANS

James Cook
(1728–1779)

EARLY YEARS

Navigator and explorer James Cook was born in 1728 in Yorkshire, England. He grew up on a farm, but at the age of 18 he was apprenticed to a merchant seaman. In 1755 Cook enlisted in the British Royal Navy and soon showed a talent for mapmaking, surveying and navigating.

In 1756, during the Seven Years' War, Cook was promoted to the position of Master. He was appointed King's Surveyor in 1763.

FIRST VOYAGE (1768–1771)

In 1768 Cook was chosen to lead his first expedition on behalf of the King of England. His mission was to travel to Tahiti to chart the transit of the planet Venus across the sun. Once this mission was complete, he was to travel south in search of new land.

In August 1768, Cook and his crew set sail on board the HMB *Endeavour*. After completing their mission in Tahiti in June 1769, Captain Cook and his crew continued south. They were in search of *Terra Australis*, a great southern Land that was rumoured to exist.

From 1769 to 1770 Cook circumnavigated New Zealand, making the first complete map of that coastline. Finally, in April 1770, the *Endeavour* reached the east coast of Australia, which was then known as New Holland. While travelling north along the Great Barrier Reef, the *Endeavour* was almost shipwrecked.

On 22 August 1770, Captain James Cook raised the British flag on Possession Island and claimed the east coast of Australia for King George III of England. The *Endeavour* set sail for home, arriving back in England in July 1771, nearly three years after its departure.

SECOND VOYAGE (1772–1775)

Even though Cook had already mapped the east coast of Australia, people weren't sure this was the great *Terra Australis*. So Cook was given a new mission – to find *Terra Australis* or prove that it was not there at all. Cook took two ships, the *Adventure* and the *Resolution*, and sailed below 70 degrees latitude, the furthest south any European had ever been. Cook charted many Pacific Ocean Islands along the way, including Easter Island, Fiji and the New Hebrides, but no new land was found.

FINAL VOYAGE (1776–1779)

In 1776 Captain Cook commanded the HMS *Resolution* on a search for a northwest passage between the Atlantic and the Pacific via the Arctic. He discovered Christmas Island and the Hawaiian Islands, charted the Pacific North Coast of America and crossed the Arctic Circle. On the return journey, the *Resolution* stopped again in Hawaii to carry out repairs. On 14 February 1779, Captain James Cook was killed in a dispute with the Hawaiians.

Arthur Phillip

BORN·1738   DIED·1814

First Governor of New South Wales Arthur Phillip was born in London in 1738. Phillip was apprenticed to the Royal British Navy at the age of 13. In 1786 he was chosen to govern the first British penal settlement on the east coast of Australia. He sailed to Australia as Commander of the First Fleet and arrived in Port Jackson, now referred to as Sydney Harbour, in January 1788. Phillip named the settlement Sydney and remained as Governor until December 1792.

Joseph Banks
(1743–1820)

EARLY YEARS

Botanist Joseph Banks was born into a wealthy family in Westminster, England. While he was at college, Banks developed a love of science, history and botany. When his father died, Banks received a large inheritance and decided to leave Oxford University without finishing his degree. He chose to devote his life to natural science instead.

In 1766 Banks joined an expedition to Newfoundland and Labrador in Canada so he could study the natural history of the region. In the same year, he was elected a fellow of the Royal Society of London for Improving Natural Knowledge.

VOYAGE OF THE HMB *ENDEAVOUR*

In 1768 Banks was chosen to join an expedition bound for Tahiti and the unmapped lands of the southern ocean. The expedition, commanded by Captain James Cook, set sail from England on board the HMB *Endeavour*. They journeyed to Tahiti to chart the transit of the planet Venus across the sun, and then continued southwards, where they mapped the coast of New Zealand. Banks collected and recorded botanical specimens along the way.

In April 1770 the crew on board the *Endeavour* became the first Europeans to discover the east coast of Australia. They set anchor at what was to become Botany Bay, a name Captain Cook chose because of all the new plant species that Joseph Banks found and collected there.

The expedition spent seven weeks near Cooktown in Queensland while a hole in the ship's hull was repaired. During this stopover Banks collected many samples of native trees and flowers to take home to England. As well as collecting specimens, Banks kept journals of his general impressions of the Australian east coast and the plants, insects, molluscs, reptiles, birds and fish he found. These

**NOTABLE
HONOURS & AWARDS**
Knighthood (1781)

journals were to become the first recorded introduction of many new species to the western world, including eucalyptus, acacia, mimosa and Banksia (named after Joseph Banks).

The discoveries made Banks famous on his return to England and in 1778 he was elected President of the Royal Society, a position he would hold for 41 years. About 80 species of Australian plants carry Banks' name.

John Macarthur

BORN ▪ 1767   DIED ▪ 1834

John Macarthur introduced Merino sheep to Australia and is considered the pioneer of our national wool industry. Macarthur also played a leading role in early Australian politics and architecture. Born in Plymouth, Britain, he was posted to New South Wales in 1789 as a member of the British Army.

" With the first day light this morn the Land was seen, at 10 it was pretty plainly to be observd; it made in sloping hills, coverd in Part with trees or bushes, but interspersd with large tracts of sand. At Noon the land much the same. "

– From the Endeavour journal of Joseph Banks

Matthew Flinders
(1774–1814)

EARLY YEARS

Explorer and navigator Matthew Flinders was born and educated in Donington in Lincolnshire, England. Flinders joined the British Navy at the age of 15, determined to live a life of adventure and exploration.

CIRCUMNAVIGATION

In 1795 Flinders visited New Holland (the name Dutchman Abel Tasman had given Australia) for the first time as part of a Navy expedition to Port Jackson in New South Wales. During the long sea voyage from England on the HMS *Reliance* Flinders made friends with George Bass, the ship's surgeon.

On a later expedition in 1798, Flinders, who was now a Lieutenant in the Navy, sailed with George Bass across the body of water that later became known as Bass Strait and confirmed that Van Diemen's Land (Tasmania) was an island.

By 1801, Flinders had developed a reputation as one of the leading navigators of his time and was promoted to the position of Commander. He was asked to chart the whole coastline of New Holland. By 1803, Flinders had completed his circumnavigation of the continent and set sail for England.

IMPRISONMENT

On his way back to England, Flinders was forced to drop anchor at Mauritius (then a French-governed island in the Indian Ocean) for ship repairs. At that time, Britain and France were at war but Flinders thought that because he was engaged in scientific work he would be considered harmless. But the Governor arrested him and his crew, and kept them imprisoned for more than six years. While he was held captive, Flinders wrote down everything that had happened on his voyages, including all his reasons for giving New Holland the name 'Australia', in the hope of publishing his notes when he was released. By the time Flinders was released and returned to England, he was weakened by his years as a prisoner and died before his important book and atlas *A Voyage to Terra Australis* was published.

AUSTRALIA

It is likely Flinders borrowed the word 'Australia' from early records, where it was used to refer to the whole South Pacific region. But Flinders used this name or *Terra Australis* (Great South Land) to refer to only the island continent of New Holland. After years of discussion (and after Flinders' death), Governor Macquarie recommended to the Colonial Office that the name 'Australia' be officially adopted. The British Admiralty agreed in 1824.

George Bass
BORN ▪ 1771   DIED ▪ 1803

Ship's surgeon and explorer George Bass sailed around Tasmania (originally called Van Diemen's Land) with Matthew Flinders. Flinders was so impressed with the notes Bass made during their expedition that he asked Governor John Hunter to name the stretch of water between Tasmania and the Australian mainland after Bass.

❝ There are few things more pleasing than the contemplation of order and useful arrangement . . . perhaps this satisfaction cannot be anywhere more fully enjoyed than where a settlement of civilised people is fixing itself upon a newly discovered or savage coast. ❞

– Admiral Arthur Phillip

Edward John Eyre
(1815–1901)

EARLY YEARS

Pioneer farmer and explorer Edward John Eyre was born in Bedfordshire, England. Instead of enlisting in the Army or going to college, Eyre immigrated to Australia when he was 17 years old. He arrived in Sydney but soon moved to the Hunter River district in the hope of learning how to manage sheep and cattle. Within a year, Eyre had bought 400 lambs.

CROSSING SOUTH AUSTRALIA

Eyre wanted be the first to bring cattle overland from Sydney to Adelaide, so in 1838 he made the journey with 1,000 sheep and 600 cattle.

Once he got to Adelaide, Eyre made a good profit from the sale of the sheep and cattle, and used the money to fund an expedition to the inland areas of South Australia. He became the first European to cross southern Australia from east to west, travelling more than 3,000 kilometres across the Nullarbor Plain from Adelaide to Albany.

LATER YEARS

From 1848 to 1853, Eyre was Lieutenant-Governor of a province of New Zealand, and from 1954 he was Governor of several Caribbean island colonies. Later in life he returned to the United Kingdom, where he died.

Lake Eyre, Eyre Peninsula, Eyre Creek and Eyre Highway (the main highway from South Australia to Western Australia) are all named after the explorer.

> **"If there is any road not travelled then that is the one I must take."**
>
> – *Edward John Eyre*

> **"The consumers' wants in a wheat are that its flour be nutritious and strength sustaining and capable of being made into a loaf which is light, white, and so attractive to the eye, agreeable to eat, and easy to digest."**
>
> *– William Farrer*

Hume & Hovell

BORN ▪ 1797   DIED ▪ 1873; BORN ▪ 1786   DIED ▪ 1875

In October 1824, Hamilton Hume and William Hovell led an expedition to find new farmland in the south of the colony of New South Wales. The expedition went from Appin in New South Wales to what is now known as Corio Bay in Victoria, opening up vast areas of new grazing land. The Hume Highway between Sydney and Melbourne is named after Hamilton Hume.

Hamilton Hume

William Hovell

William Farrer

BORN ▪ 1845 DIED ▪ 1906

William Farrer is known as 'the father of the Australian wheat industry'. He bred the 'Federation' strain of wheat and worked to improve the quality and quantity of Australia's national wheat harvest. After its introduction in 1903, the Federation wheat strain trebled Australia's wheat harvest over the next twenty years.

Gregory Blaxland
(1778–1853)

EARLY YEARS

Explorer and pioneer farmer Gregory Blaxland was born in Kent, England. The Blaxland family were friends with the famous botanist Joseph Banks, who influenced Blaxland and his brother to immigrate to Australia. The government promised the brothers free passage as well as land and convict servants if they took up farming in Australia. So in 1805 Blaxland travelled to Australia with his wife, children and brother John. Blaxland obtained land near Eastwood in Sydney. He bought cows and sheep and started producing meat and wool.

CROSSING THE BLUE MOUNTAINS

Keen to find new pastures for his stock, Blaxland made several attempts to cross the Blue Mountains, before asking Governor Macquarie for permission to form an exploration party.

In 1813, Blaxland set off with William Lawson and William Charles Wentworth on a journey over the mountains known as the Great Dividing Range (the Blue Mountains being part of this). Their aim was to open up a route for settlers to cross and farm the land on the other side of the range.

The expedition included a local guide, convict servants, packhorses and dogs.

After 21 days they reached the summit of what is now known as Mount Blaxland. They saw below them forest and grassland suitable for raising stock and supporting settlers. Hungry and ill, they returned home without actually crossing to the other side, but they had opened up a path for others to follow.

William Lawson

BORN▪1774   DIED▪1850

English-born explorer and landholder William Lawson accompanied Blaxland and Wentworth on the first recorded crossing of the Blue Mountains. In 1819 Lawson became commandant of the new settlement of Bathurst in New South Wales, a position he kept until 1824.

William Charles Wentworth

BORN▪1790   DIED▪1872

Explorer, landowner, author, barrister and statesman William Charles Wentworth accompanied Blaxland and Lawson on the first European crossing of the Blue Mountains. Wentworth was one of the first native-born Australians to earn an international reputation and was a leading campaigner for self-government for the Australian colonies. He was also instrumental in establishing the first real system of state primary education.

> **"It has changed the aspect of the colony, from a confined insulated tract of land, to a rich and extensive continent."**
>
> *– Gregory Blaxland on his expedition across the Blue Mountains*

KEY ACHIEVEMENT
Father of Australian Federation

Henry Parkes
(1815–1896)

EARLY YEARS

Politician and journalist Henry Parkes was born in Warwickshire, England. In 1839 Parkes and his young family immigrated to New South Wales, in the hope of finding a better life in the new colony. Parkes worked initially as a farm labourer and a public servant, but by 1845 he had started an ivory-turning and import business in Sydney. As a businessman, Parkes began to take an interest in the political affairs of the colony.

POLITICAL LIFE

Throughout the 1840s Parkes wrote articles about politics for various newspapers and journals. He was known for his radical views, particularly about land reform, stopping convict transportation, constitutional reform and universal suffrage (the right to vote). In 1849 Parkes made his first public speech on the topic of universal suffrage, and in 1850 he founded his own newspaper, *The Empire*.

In 1854 Parkes was elected to parliament and campaigned for better conditions for the working class, as well as more education facilities and a bold new railway system. In 1856 Parkes was forced to resign from parliament to focus on *The Empire* newspaper. He briefly re-entered parliament in 1858, but was again forced to resign when *The Empire* went into bankruptcy. Parkes was again elected to parliament from 1859 to 1860, this time as a representative for East Sydney.

In January 1864 Parkes won the seat of Kiama in New South Wales, which he held until 1870, before he was again forced to resign due to financial difficulties. In 1871 Parkes was re-elected to parliament and in 1872 he became Premier of New South Wales. Parkes was thrown out as Premier in 1875, when the general public disagreed with him and the governor about the length of bushranger Frank Gardiner's jail sentence. Parkes was re-elected Premier in December 1877 and went on to serve for five terms.

FEDERATION

From the late 1880s, Parkes worked hard to gather political and public support for Federation: the unification of Australian colonies to form one nation. Parkes was the main supporter of Federation in New South Wales, the largest colony at the time of the final referendums, but the one where there was the least support for the idea of unification.

"Our cause is peace. Our cause is the consolidation of Australian interests. One people. One destiny."

– Henry Parkes on Federation

Robert O'Hara Burke

William John Wills

Burke & Wills

BORN▪1821   DIED▪1861; BORN▪1834   DIED▪1861
CATEGORY: EXPLORATION

In 1860 Robert O'Hara Burke led 19 men on the first European expedition across Australia from Melbourne in the south to the Gulf of Carpentaria in the far north. William John Wills joined the expedition as surveyor and astronomer, but was promoted to the position of second-in-command when a number of men resigned from the mission after the first month. The remaining men successfully completed the expedition from south to north, but both Burke and Wills died on the return journey, along with all but one member of the team.

Mary MacKillop
(1842–1909)

EARLY YEARS

Australia's first saint Mary MacKillop was born in Fitzroy, Victoria. MacKillop attended private schools as a child, and was also taught by her father, who had studied for the Catholic priesthood. Throughout her teenage years, MacKillop worked as a shopgirl, governess and teacher to help her family financially.

TEACHING

In 1861 MacKillop met Father Julian Tenison Woods and they soon became friends. Three years later she opened a boarding school for girls, the Bay View House Seminary for Young Ladies, in Portland, Victoria. In 1865 Father Woods invited MacKillop, along with her sisters Annie and Lexie, to set up a Catholic school in Penola, South Australia with the aim of making education accessible for all children.

SISTERS OF ST JOSEPH

In March 1866 the first St Joseph's school opened in Penola. It was during this period that MacKillop declared her devotion to God and in 1867 she took her formal religious vows, becoming Sister Mary of the Cross, as well as the first Sister and Mother Superior of the Order of the Sisters of St Joseph of the Sacred Heart (the Josephites).

By 1869 the Josephites had established 17 schools, educating more than 1,600 children from poor backgrounds. The Josephite communities continued to expand to Queensland.

But in 1871 MacKillop was excommunicated after conflict between the Order and Bishop Sheil of Adelaide, who wanted to place St Joseph convents under the control of local priests, rather than allowing the Order to run independently. He revoked the excommunication a year later, a few days before his death.

In 1873 MacKillop travelled to Rome to seek approval of the rules of the Josephite Order from the Pope. She returned to Australia in 1874 and became Superior-General of the Sisterhood, opening up more schools, convents and educational institutions throughout the country. Pope Leo XVIII gave the final approval to the Sisters of St Joseph of the Sacred Heart in 1885.

MacKillop passed away in 1909, aged 67.

AUSTRALIA'S FIRST SAINT

On 19 January 1995, MacKillop was beatified by Pope John Paul II. She was canonised by Pope Benedict XVI on 17 October 2010, and became the only Australian to be officially recognised as a saint by the Catholic Church.

"We must teach more by example than by word."

– Saint Mary MacKillop

KEY ACHIEVEMENT
Improved conditions for poor women and immigrants

Caroline Chisholm
(1808–1877)

EARLY YEARS

Women's rights advocate Caroline Chisholm was born into a wealthy family in Northampton, England. From a young age her parents taught her about the importance of helping people who were not as fortunate as she was.

CAMPAIGNING FOR WOMEN AND IMMIGRANTS

In 1830 Chisholm married Archibald, who was an army officer of the East India Company. Archibald was posted to Madras in India in 1832 and Chisholm joined him a year later. In India, Chisholm noticed the wives and daughters of British soldiers were living in poverty and were often forced into prostitution to support themselves. In 1834 Chisholm established the Female School of Industry for the wives of European soldiers. Her goal was to provide them with basic literacy, numeracy and domestic skills.

In 1838 the Chisholms moved to New South Wales, where Caroline continued her work improving the lives of poor immigrant women. She opened a women's refuge in an old army barracks in Sydney and asked wealthy colonists to donate funds to keep it open.

Chisholm helped to find employment for poor, single women in domestic service roles. She also worked to place more white women in employment in the outback, campaigning for better conditions for them as well as for Aboriginal women.

The Chisholms moved back to England in 1846, but Caroline continued to advocate for the rights of migrant women and poor families in Australia.

Edith Cowan
(1861–1932)

KEY ACHIEVEMENT
First woman elected to the Australian parliament

EARLY YEARS

Women's rights campaigner and politician Edith Cowan was born in Geraldton, Western Australia. When Cowan was seven her mother died in childbirth and her father sent her to a boarding school in Perth, which was run by the Cowan sisters.

Cowan left boarding school at the age of fifteen and finished her schooling with ex-headmistress Canon Sweeting, who is credited with fostering Cowan's love of books and reading.

FIGHTING FOR WOMEN'S RIGHTS

In 1879 Edith married James Cowan, brother of her former teachers, and registrar and master of the Supreme Court. This gave her insight into the living conditions of disadvantaged groups in society. She became increasingly concerned about women's rights in particular.

In 1894 Cowan helped found the Karrakatta Club, the first women's club in Australia. The club encouraged its members to educate themselves in order to expand their future prospects. The group actively campaigned to give women the right to vote, which they were granted in Western Australia in 1899.

Cowan was also interested in women's health and worked hard to encourage the building of Perth's King Edward Memorial Hospital for Women, which opened in 1916.

POLITICAL LIFE

In 1920 Cowan stood as a Nationalist candidate in the federal election and became the first woman elected to the Australian parliament. She championed women's rights, advocating for increased opportunities for women in the workforce and introducing sex education in schools. Although she lost her seat four years later and never regained it, Cowan remained involved in social issues for the rest of her life.

Douglas Mawson
(1882–1958)

EARLY YEARS

Antarctic explorer Douglas Mawson was born in Yorkshire, England. He moved to Australia with his family when he was two years old. Mawson attended the University of Sydney when he was 16. After graduating with a degree in mining engineering, he became a lecturer in the origin and structure of rocks at the University of Adelaide. Mawson often took his students on trips to the Flinders Ranges, which were formed by glaciers millions of years ago, but he was keen to explore Antarctica, where glaciers still existed.

WORKING WITH SIR ERNEST SHACKLETON

In 1907 Ernest Shackleton, leader of the British Antarctic Expedition, visited Adelaide on his way south to the Antarctic. His mission was to reach the South Magnetic Pole. Mawson asked if he could join Shackleton and was appointed physicist for the duration of the expedition. The expedition was successful, and Mawson made a number of valuable scientific observations along the way.

FIRST AUSTRALASIAN ANTARCTIC EXPEDITION

In 1911, Mawson led the first Australasian expedition to the coast of Antarctica nearest Australia, which was largely unexplored. The expedition sailed to Antarctica on the SY *Aurora* and set up a main base in Commonwealth Bay. A second base was made on an ice shelf in Queen Mary Land. In the spring of 1912 Mawson and two colleagues, along with a team of huskies to pull their sleds, set off from the second base to survey King George V Land. Mawson, Xavier Mertz and Lieutenant Belgrave Ninnis made good progress mapping the coast, discovering glaciers and other landmarks, and collecting samples of rock.

But then disaster struck. The winter that year was harsh, with almost constant blizzards. Lieutenant Ninnis fell down a crevasse with his team of dogs and most of the food supplies. Although Mawson and his remaining colleague started back to the hut, they had nothing to eat and were forced to kill their dogs for food. Both men grew increasingly weak and Mertz deteriorated to the point where he could barely leave his tent. He died on 8 January 1913 after falling into a coma.

Mawson struggled on alone, nearly perishing a number of times before finally reaching safety. Mawson's extraordinary solo journey and survival in extreme conditions is considered a landmark of polar exploration. In 1914 Mawson received a knighthood in recognition of his Antarctic findings. Mawson remained passionate about the Antarctic and led two more voyages to the region, resulting in Australia claiming 42 percent of the continent.

NOTABLE HONOURS & AWARDS

Royal Geographical Society's Antarctic Medal (1909)

Knighthood (1914)

Royal Geographical Society Founder's Medal (1915)

Order of the British Empire (1920)

Fellow of the Royal Society (1923)

Foundation Fellow, Australian Academy of Science (1954)

"We had discovered an accursed country. We had found the Home of the Blizzard."

— Douglas Mawson

Adelaide Miethke

BORN · 1881   DIED · 1962

Educator and teacher Adelaide Miethke played a key role in the formation of the School of the Air, which put children in outback Australia in direct touch with their teachers and fellow pupils. Miethke was appointed an Officer of the Order of the British Empire in 1937 for her outstanding contribution to education.

Vida Goldstein

BORN · 1869   DIED · 1949

One of Australia's first female politicians and feminists, Vida Goldstein campaigned during the 1890s for women in Australia to be given the right to vote. Thanks to the work of Goldstein and her fellow suffragettes, in 1902 the Commonwealth Parliament passed the Commonwealth Franchise Act, which allowed women to vote and to stand for election in the Federal Parliament. Goldstein spent the rest of her life campaigning for the rights of women across all areas of society.

> **"We have embarked on a new age of chivalry – the chivalry of women towards women."**
>
> *– Vida Goldstein*

Lawrence Hargrave

BORN ▪ 1850   DIED ▪ 1915

Lawrence Hargrave was an English-born inventor and a pioneer of power-controlled flight. Hargrave's most notable achievement was his invention of the box kite, also known as a cellular kite, because several boxes could be linked together to give greater lift. This kite, created in 1893, was used as a basis for aircraft designed by early European builders. The first power-controlled flight in Europe in 1906 was acknowledged to have been inspired by Hargrave's box kite.

John Duigan

BORN ▪ 1882   DIED ▪ 1951

Pioneer aviator John Duigan built and flew the first Australian-designed aeroplane. Duigan built a bi-plane powered by a four-cylinder engine and made a short flight in 1910. A longer flight in the same year was Duigan's first real success and he followed this with increasingly longer and higher flights. His younger brother, Reg, helped him build and test the bi-plane and often piloted it himself. In May 1911, Duigan flew the plane in public at Bendigo Racecourse, where it completed a full circuit of the area. He received the Military Cross for gallantry in an air fight in the First World War.

Bert Hinkler

BORN ▪ 1892   DIED ▪ 1933

Inventor and pioneer aviator Bert Hinkler was known as the Australian Lone Eagle. He was the first person to fly solo from England to Australia in 1928, as well as across the southern Atlantic Ocean in 1931. In January 1933, Hinkler left London on a mission to break the flying record to Australia. His body was found later that year in the mountains of Italy, where his plane had crashed.

KEY ACHIEVEMENT
Piloted the first trans-Pacific flight from the United States to Australia

Charles Kingsford Smith
(1897–1935)

EARLY YEARS

Aviator Charles Kingsford Smith was born in Hamilton, Queensland. When he was 18, Kingsford Smith enlisted in the Australian Army and during the First World War he was sent to Gallipoli. He served as a motorcycle despatch rider, before becoming a pilot and transferring to the Royal Flying Corps in 1917. Later that year, Kingsford Smith was injured when his plane was shot down. He was awarded the Military Cross for his gallantry in battle and was sent home to Australia to recover. He then served as an instructor for the Royal Flying Corps in England.

AFTER THE WAR

After the war Kingsford Smith operated a joy-flight business in England before travelling to America and then back home to Australia, where he again operated joy-flights.

Believing there was a great deal of potential for air transport in Australia, Kingsford Smith applied for a commercial pilot's licence in 1921 and became one of the country's first airline pilots.

NOTABLE HONOURS & AWARDS

Order of the Military Cross (1917)

Air Force Cross – United Kingdom (1927)

Knight Bachelor (1932)

THE FIRST TRANS-PACIFIC FLIGHT FROM THE UNITED STATES TO AUSTRALIA

In June 1927, Kingsford Smith and fellow pilot Charles Ulm completed a round-Australia circuit in only ten days and 5 hours. Inspired by this feat, they began to plan the first trans-Pacific flight from the United States to Australia.

In 1928, Kingsford Smith and a four-man crew left California in a monoplane named the *Southern Cross* in a bid to complete the first trans-Pacific flight to Australia. The flight was a triumph and the team landed in Brisbane to be met by 26,000 cheering fans.

TRANS-TASMAN FLIGHT

Later in 1928, Kingsford Smith and Ulm made the first non-stop flight across Australia and decided to attempt the Tasman crossing to New Zealand, which had never before been successfully completed. Despite unfavourable weather conditions, they set off with two additional crewmembers and landed safely in Christchurch, where a welcoming crowd of 30,000 people greeted them.

LATER FLIGHTS

In 1934, Kingsford Smith purchased the *Lady Southern Cross* and flew her from Australia to the United States, completing the first eastward crossing of the Pacific Ocean by plane.

DISAPPEARANCE

In 1935, Kingsford Smith and his co-pilot were flying the *Lady Southern Cross* overnight from India to Singapore in an attempt to break the England–Australia speed record, when they disappeared over the Andaman Sea never to be seen again.

The Kingsford Smith Memorial in Brisbane is home to Kingsford Smith's most famous aircraft, the *Southern Cross*, where it is on permanent display. The Kingsford Smith International Airport in Sydney is named after him, with the federal electorate surrounding the airport named the Division of Kingsford Smith.

"We seemed to be leaving the world for a new one of our own. Before us swept an immensity of silent ocean."

– Charles Kingsford Smith

Nancy Bird-Walton
(1915–2009)

EARLY YEARS

Aviatrix Nancy Bird-Walton was born in Kew, New South Wales. From a very early age she dreamed of flying an aeroplane. Bird-Walton was forced to leave school at age 13 to help her family earn money during the Great Depression. Four years later, Charles Kingsford Smith opened a flying school near Sydney and Bird-Walton became one of his first pupils, graduating in 1934. At only 19, Bird-Walton was the youngest woman in the British Commonwealth to get a commercial pilots' licence.

FLYING MEDICAL SERVICE

In 1935 Bird-Walton's father helped her buy her first aircraft, a Gipsy Moth, and she soon took off on a tour of regional Australia, alongside co-pilot Peggy McKillop. Along the way Bird-Walton met the Reverend Stanley Drummond, who hired her to help set up and operate a flying medical service in outback New South Wales called the Far West Children's Health Scheme. In the early days she used her own small plane as an air ambulance.

AUSTRALIAN WOMEN PILOTS' ASSOCIATION

Bird-Walton entered an air race from Adelaide to Brisbane in 1936 and won the Ladies' Trophy. She helped train women pilots in the Second World War, and in 1950 she became the founder and patron of the Australian Women Pilots' Association.

NOTABLE HONOURS & AWARDS

Officer of the Order of the British Empire (1966)

Officer of the Order of Australia (1990)

Australian Living Treasure (1997)

Herbert Cole 'Nugget' Coombs

BORN ▪ 1906   DIED ▪ 1997

Australian economist and public servant Herbert Coombs served as the first Governor of the Reserve Bank of Australia (Australia's central bank from 1960, responsible for issuing the nation's banknotes). In 1968 he retired as a public servant, having advised seven prime ministers on economic matters during the course of his career.

"You haven't seen Australia unless you've seen it from the air."

– Nancy Bird-Walton

As well as his many other achievements, inventor **LAWRENCE HARGRAVE** also built a compressed air engine that was used to power French aircraft during the First World War.

During **Douglas Mawson's** Australasian Antarctic expedition, his colleague is believed to have died from the toxins in the sled dogs' livers, which the men were forced to eat for survival.

CAPTAIN JAMES COOK is said to have brought lots of **FRESH FRUIT** on board his expeditions to ward off outbreaks of **SCURVY** amongst his **CREW**.

IT'S BELIEVED AVIATOR **CHARLES KINGSFORD SMITH** WAS ONE OF THE FIRST PEOPLE RESCUED BY A LIFESAVER USING A REEL, ROPE AND BELT ON BONDI BEACH IN 1907.

During the First World War, aviator **BERT HINKLER** became an expert gunner and developed a dual-control system that allowed gunners to take over from disabled pilots.

Explorer ~~GREGORY BLAXLAND~~ was one of the first settlers to plant grapes for **WINEMAKING** and he found a species resistant to a plant disease called **blight**. He took samples of his wine on his trips to England in 1822 and 1826 and won **MEDALS** for it both times.

Father of Federation **HENRY PARKES** was said to be a keen collector of autographs, as well as native wild animals.

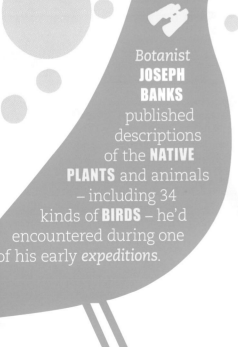

Botanist **JOSEPH BANKS** published descriptions of the **NATIVE PLANTS** and animals – including 34 kinds of **BIRDS** – he'd encountered during one of his early *expeditions*.

Explorer **MATTHEW FLINDERS** took his faithful cat, Trim, (who was born on the way to BOTANY BAY in 1799) with him on his voyages from 1801 to 1803.

"The pursuit of knowledge is far more important than even knowledge itself."

– John Curtin

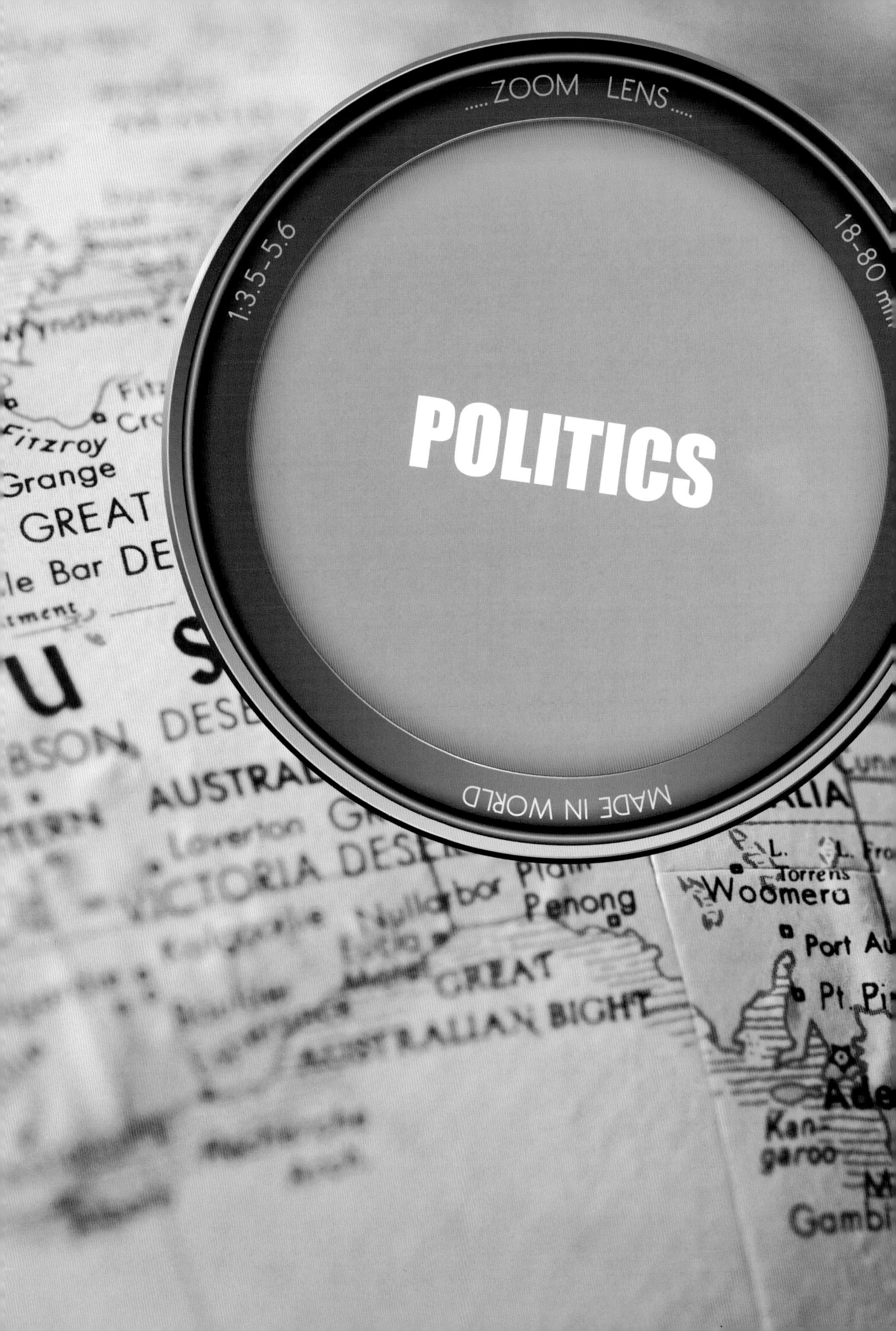
ZOOM LENS
1:3.5-5.6
18-80 mm
MADE IN WORLD
Fitzroy
Grange
GREAT
Bar DE
Woomera
Torrens
Penong
Port Au
Pt. Pi
GREAT
AUSTRALIAN BIGHT
VICTORIA DESE
AUSTRAL
Kan-
garoo
Gambi

POLITICS

Edmund Barton
(1849–1920)

EARLY YEARS

Australia's first prime minister Edmund Barton was born in Glebe, New South Wales. Barton attended Fort Street High School and then Sydney Grammar School, where he was both dux and School Captain. After excelling at school, Barton won the University Medal in Classics from the University of Sydney. In 1871 he became a barrister.

FEDERATION

Barton developed an interest in politics and stood for New South Wales State Parliament a number of times, before winning a seat in 1879.

Throughout the 1890s Barton was intrumental in bringing about the Federation – the unification of Australian states and territories under one central government.

PRIME MINISTER AND FOUNDING JUDGE

Following Federation and the establishment of the Commonwealth of Australia in 1901, Barton contested the first ever federal election. As Barton was the head of the Protectionist Party, a popular native-born Australian, and because no single party had won a majority, the Governor-General asked Barton to serve as prime minister and to form a cabinet until new elections could be held.

Barton resigned from the position of Prime Minister of Australia in 1903 and became a judge on Australia's High Court, serving there until he died.

NOTABLE HONOURS & AWARDS

Knight Grand Cross of St Michael and St George (1902)

Grand Cordon, Order of the Rising Sun (1905)

Alfred Deakin
(1856–1919)

KEY ACHIEVEMENT
Second Prime Minister of Australia and a leader of the movement for Australian Federation

EARLY YEARS

Politician, barrister and journalist Alfred Deakin was born in Collingwood, Victoria. He attended the University of Melbourne, where he studied law. Deakin was also interested in journalism and in 1880 he became editor of *The Leader*.

FEDERATION

Deakin was elected to the Victorian Parliament in 1880. He became involved in public water supply, introducing laws to nationalise water rights and providing state aid for irrigation projects, which played a major part in establishing irrigation in Australia.

During the 1890s, Deakin helped draft a constitution for the proposed Federation of Australian states and territories, ensuring it was fair to all Australians. When Edmund Barton retired as prime minister in 1903, Deakin succeeded him and helped to establish an effective Commonwealth government. Deakin appointed more judges to the High Court, provided funding to buy ships for the newly established Royal Australian Navy and merged his Protectionist Party with another party to create the Commonwealth Liberal Party (CLP). The CLP went on to become the modern Liberal Party of Australia.

> **❝Creating a nation requires the will of the people.❞**
>
> – *Edmund Barton on Federation*

Billy Hughes
(1862–1952)

EARLY YEARS

Politician Billy Hughes was born in London and immigrated to Australia when he was 22. He found work as a labourer in the Sydney suburb of Balmain and then worked in a pharmacy before opening his own small shop. Hughes joined the Socialist League in 1892 and was involved in the establishment of the Australian Workers' Union.

POLITICAL LIFE

Hughes was a controversial, larger-than-life politician who spent 51 years in Federal Parliament. He switched political parties five times throughout his career. He was first a member of the Labor Party (1901–16), then National Labor (1916–17), then Nationalist (1917–30), then Australian (1930–31), then United Australia (1931–44) and finally Liberal (1944–52). He was still working and an active member of parliament when he died aged 90, the longest-serving member in Australia's history.

TREATY OF VERSAILLES

Hughes served as Prime Minister of Australia from 1915 to 1923, which covered the period of the First World War (1914–1918). One of the high points of his time as prime minister came in 1919, when he travelled to Paris to attend the Versailles Peace Conference. The conference had been called to decide the fate of Germany, who had been defeated in the war. After 16 months of negotiation between delegates from 27 nations, Hughes signed the Treaty of Versailles on behalf of Australia. It was the first international treaty Australia had ever signed. The League of Nations was also formed at this time as an international body to maintain world peace. Hughes requested that Australia have its own independent representation within the League.

NOTABLE HONOURS & AWARDS

Member of the Order of the Companions of Honour (1941)

Queen's Counsel (1919)

Robert Menzies
(1894–1978)

EARLY YEARS

Politician and lawyer Robert Menzies was born in Jeparit, Victoria. He began his education in a one-room school, later studying law at the University of Melbourne.

POLITICAL LIFE

Menzies was one of Australia's leading lawyers before entering the Victorian Parliament in 1928. Six years later, he won a seat in Federal Parliament and served as Attorney-General in the United Australia Party government of Joseph Lyons.

Menzies was prime minister twice, from 1939 to 1941 and from 1949 to 1966. His first time in office followed the death of his former leader Joseph Lyons. He then spent eight years in opposition and founded the Liberal Party of Australia during that time.

During his second term as prime minister, Menzies signed the Australia, New Zealand, United States Security Treaty (ANZUS) and the South-East Asia Treaty Organisation (SEATO) treaty. He also sent Australian troops to support American-led forces fighting in Korea, and committed Australian combat forces to fight alongside their American allies in the Vietnam War.

Menzies resigned as prime minister in 1966. He is the last Australian prime minister to have left office on his own terms.

NOTABLE HONOURS & AWARDS

King's Counsel (1929)

Privy Councillor (1937)

US League of Merit (1950)

Member of the Order of the Companions of Honour (1951)

Order of the Thistle (1963)

Warden of the Cinque Ports (1965)

Order of the Rising Sun, First Class (1973)

Knight of the Order of Australia (1976)

> **❝ Never take any notice of anonymous letters, unless you get a few thousand on the same subject. ❞**
>
> *– Robert Menzies*

KEY ACHIEVEMENT
Led Australia as Prime Minister during the Second World War

John Curtin
(1885–1945)

EARLY YEARS

Politician and journalist John Curtin was born in Creswick, Victoria. He left school at the age of 13 to help support his family. Curtin developed an interest in politics during his teens and started attending a weekly study group held by local State member Frank Anstey. He also began writing articles for various left-wing newspapers.

POLITICAL LIFE

In 1911 Curtin became secretary of the Victorian branch of the Timberworkers' Union and fought hard for improved work and living conditions for its members. In 1914 he became the first federal president of the union. In September that year Curtin ran unsuccessfully as the Labor candidate for the seat of Balaclava in Melbourne, campaigning against compulsory conscription in the First World War.

Curtin moved to Perth in 1917 and became editor of the Labor Party's journal, the *Westralian Worker*. In 1928 he ran as the Labor candidate for the seat of Fremantle and won by a large majority. After losing this seat in 1931, Curtin again worked as a journalist for three years. He regained the seat of Fremantle in the 1934 election.

In 1935 Curtin was elected as leader of the Labor Party and leader of the Opposition. In September 1939 the outbreak of the Second World War was declared, and issues of national security became increasingly important. In 1940 Curtin led the Labor Party to a narrow victory in the federal election. They formed a minority government and Curtin was sworn in as the 14th Prime Minister of Australia.

SECOND WORLD WAR

In December 1941 Japan attacked Pearl Harbour in the United States. Australia was also under threat of Japanese invasion and in February 1942 that threat became reality when Japanese fighter planes dropped bombs on Darwin. Curtin called on Australia's two main allies, the United States and Great Britain, for help and brought home two divisions of Australian soldiers from the Middle East to strengthen the domestic front. He did so against the wishes of British Prime Minister Winston Churchill.

Curtin was re-elected at the 1943 federal election in a huge outburst of support for Labor. He died of a heart attack in July 1945, less than two months before the Allies claimed victory at the end of the Second World War.

"One of the greatest Australians ever."

– Former Prime Minister Arthur Fadden on John Curtin

KEY ACHIEVEMENT
Instrumental in the formation of the United Nations

Herbert Vere Evatt (1894–1965)

EARLY YEARS

Politician, lawyer and judge Herbert Vere Evatt was born in Maitland, New South Wales. He excelled at school and won scholarships to the University of Sydney, where he was awarded the University Medal twice, for philosophy and law.

HIGH COURT JUDGE

After a brief career in politics, Evatt was appointed the youngest-ever justice of the High Court of Australia in 1930. Following a brilliant ten year legal career, he resigned to return to politics and was elected a federal minister in 1940.

POLITICAL LIFE

When the Australian Labor Party won the election in 1940, Evatt became Attorney-General and Minister for External Affairs (Foreign Minister). After Labor again won in the 1946 election he was appointed deputy leader under Prime Minister Ben Chifley.

Evatt held a number of strategic roles during the Second World War and in 1945 he, along with other world leaders, helped establish the United Nations (UN). He served as president of the UN General Assembly from 1948 to 1949 and helped negotiate the creation of the state of Israel. He also helped draft the United Nations Universal Declaration of Human Rights and was the first chair of the Atomic Energy Commission.

NOTABLE HONOURS & AWARDS

Queen's Counsel (1901)

In 1949 Labor lost the federal election and Evatt was elected Labor leader and leader of the Opposition, following the death of his predecessor, Ben Chifley. After being defeated in a number of elections against Liberal Prime Minister Robert Menzies, Evatt resigned from politics in 1960 to take up the position of Chief Justice of New South Wales. He retired from the bench in 1962 due to ill health.

Harold Holt
(1908–1967)

KEY ACHIEVEMENT
17th Prime Minister
of Australia

EARLY YEARS

Liberal politician Harold Holt was born in Stanmore, New South Wales. He studied law at the University of Melbourne, becoming a barrister in 1932. Holt entered Federal Parliament in 1935, and at 27 years of age was one of Australia's youngest-ever members of parliament.

POLITICAL LIFE

Holt spent 32 years in parliament, including many years as a senior cabinet minister. As Minister for Immigration from 1949 to 1956, he was responsible for relaxing the laws of the White Australia policy, thereby allowing more non-European immigrants to come to Australia.

In 1958 Holt was appointed Federal Treasurer under Liberal Prime Minister Robert Menzies. As Treasurer, Holt was instrumental in establishing the Reserve Bank of Australia as the country's central bank, and in converting Australia to decimal currency.

PRIME MINISTER

In January 1966 Robert Menzies retired as leader of the Liberal Party and Holt was sworn in as Prime Minister of Australia. He spent only 22 months in the position but oversaw some big changes, including the historic decision not to devalue the Australian dollar to match the British pound, and the 1967 referendum in which most Australians voted in favour of giving the Commonwealth power to make decisions for Indigenous Australians. Holt also decided to increase Australia's commitment in the Vietnam War and was known for his friendly relationship with American President Lyndon Baines Johnson.

On 17 December 1967, Harold Holt disappeared while swimming at Cheviot Beach in Victoria with his family. He was never seen again.

**NOTABLE
HONOURS & AWARDS**
Memeber of the Order
of the Companions
of Honour (1967)

KEY ACHIEVEMENT
21st Prime Minister
of Australia

Gough Whitlam
(1916–)

EARLY YEARS

Labor politician Gough Whitlam was born in Kew, Victoria. He studied at the University of Sydney and, after serving in the Royal Australian Air Force during the Second World War, graduated with a law degree.

POLITICAL LIFE

Whitlam joined the Australian Labor Party and entered Federal Parliament in 1952. By 1960 he was elected deputy leader of the Labor Party. In 1967 he became leader of the Labor Party and Opposition. Whitlam led his party to victory at the 1972 election and ended 23 years of Liberal-Country Coalition government.

During his time in office, Whitlam and his government made many changes to policy, including ending compulsory military conscription and the execution of criminals for federal offences, and introducing health care for all Australians, free university education and legal aid programs for people who couldn't afford a lawyer. Whitlam again won the 1974 election, but with fewer seats than before.

DISMISSAL

After the 1974 election, the Opposition won control of the Senate and, after many scandals involving government ministers and a worsening economy, the Liberal Opposition decided to challenge Whitlam. In late 1975 there was a battle when the Senate refused to pass bills releasing money the government needed in order to run. Because of the resulting stalemate, Governor-General John Kerr decided to dismiss Whitlam as prime minister. The Opposition leader, Malcolm Fraser, replaced Whitlam as prime minister. This caused a scandal, as never before in Australia's history had an elected prime minister been removed from his job by the Governer-General.

Labor suffered a landslide loss in the 1975 election, and Whitlam resigned from the Labor leadership after the party lost again at the 1977 election. When Bob Hawke became prime minister in 1983, he appointed Whitlam as ambassador to the United Nations Educational Scientific and Cultural Organization (UNESCO) in Paris, a post he held for three years.

Whitlam is an elder statesman of the Labor Party and has remained active in public life well into his nineties.

"Well may we say 'God save the Queen', because nothing will save the Governor-General."

– Gough Whitlam, on his dismissal as prime minister by the Governor-General

Neville Bonner
(1922–1999)

EARLY YEARS

Aboriginal rights campaigner and politician Neville Bonner was born on Ukerebagh Island in northern New South Wales. Bonner had little schooling, attending for only one year when he was 14. He started his working life labouring on farms and rose to become a head stockman. For 16 years he lived on an Aboriginal settlement called Palm Island with his wife and children. He took an interest in the way his people lived and was one of the community leaders on Palm Island.

ABORIGINAL RIGHTS

In 1960 Bonner and his family moved to Ipswich in Queensland. Bonner's natural leadership skills were an asset when he joined the board of directors of the One People of Australia League (OPAL), an Indigenous rights organisation that provided welfare assistance to Aboriginal people. Bonner became its Queensland president in 1970.

POLITICAL LIFE

NOTABLE HONOURS & AWARDS

Officer of the Order of Australia (1984)

Australian of the Year (1979)

In 1967, a national referendum was held to change the way Aboriginal people were treated and to give them more rights. Bonner used this opportunity to make a difference, joining the Liberal Party and entering Federal Parliament in 1971 as its first Indigenous parliamentarian. He was elected four times – in 1972, 1974, 1975 and 1980. During these years he represented his people, and through gentle persuasion helped improve the way people viewed Aboriginal rights in Australia.

Malcolm Fraser
(1930–)

KEY ACHIEVEMENT
22nd Prime Minister
of Australia

EARLY YEARS

Malcolm Fraser was born in Toorak, Victoria. He studied philosophy, politics and economics at Oxford University in England before returning to Australia to work on his family property in rural Victoria.

POLITICAL LIFE

In 1955, at the age of 25, Fraser entered Federal Parliament as its youngest member. In 1975, having held a number of senior positions in parliament, Fraser challenged the leader of his party and was appointed leader of the Opposition to take on Labor Prime Minister Gough Whitlam. The Labor Party won the 1975 election by a small minority, but the Opposition retained control of the Senate (Upper House).

THE DISMISSAL OF GOUGH WHITLAM

In October 1975, after a year of political scandals for the Labor Party, Fraser announced that his party would refuse to pass the budget bills through the Senate until Whitlam called an election. The resulting constitutional and financial crisis came to a head when the Governor-General, John Kerr, dismissed Whitlam from office on 11 November 1975 and asked Fraser to take over as prime minister. Fraser won the next election in a landslide and remained prime minister for seven-and-a-half years.

During his time in government, Fraser established the Family Court of Australia and the Federal Court of Australia in 1976, as well as the National Aboriginal Conference and the Special Broadcasting Service (SBS) in 1977. He also approved the construction of a new permanent Parliament House on Capital Hill in Canberra in 1978.

Fraser retired from parliament in 1983 but remains active in public life.

NOTABLE HONOURS & AWARDS

Member of the Order of the Companion of Honour (1977)

Companion of the Order of Australia (1988)

Australia's Human Rights Medal (2000)

Donald Chipp
(1925–2006)

EARLY YEARS

Politician Donald Chipp was born in Northcote, Victoria. He studied commerce at the University of Melbourne, served in the Royal Australian Air Force in the Second World War and helped organise the 1956 Melbourne Olympic Games.

POLITICAL LIFE

Chipp joined the Liberal Party and entered federal politics in 1960, rising quickly to a senior position and holding various portfolios as a minister under the leaderships of Harold Holt, John Gorton and Billy Snedden. In 1975 the Liberal Party came to power following the dismissal of Labor Prime Minister Gough Whitlam. But Chipp was offered a senior role in the new Liberal government.

AUSTRALIAN DEMOCRATS

NOTABLE HONOURS & AWARDS

Officer of the Order of Australia (1992)

After speaking at a number of public events alongside controversial figures of the day, such as writers Frank Hardy and Patrick White, Chipp felt he was considered a rebel by his colleagues in the Liberal Party. Disenchanted with party politics, he decided to resign from the Liberal Party in March 1977.

In December 1977 Chipp accepted an offer to become leader of a young party, the Australian Democrats, and he and a colleague were elected to the Senate that same year. As leaderof the Democrats, Chipp fought for environmental and social justice causes and helped stop the Franklin Dam project in Tasmania. By the 1980s the Democrats had risen to become a powerful force in the Senate. After spearheading this success, Chipp resigned from the Senate in 1986.

Bob Hawke
(1929–)

KEY ACHIEVEMENT
Labor Party's longest-serving Prime Minister and Australia's third-longest-serving Prime Minister

EARLY YEARS

Labor politician Bob Hawke was born in Bordertown, South Australia. He studied at Oxford University in England from 1953 to 1955 as a Rhodes Scholar. His final university thesis was on wage-fixing in Australia. Hawke returned to Australia in 1956 and became Research Officer and Advocate with the Australian Council of Trade Unions (ACTU). He was later elected as ACTU president from 1970 to 1980. Hawke's understanding of trade union issues and the fact that he was trusted by people of the working class would make a huge difference to the way he handled issues of pay and labour conditions in his later political life.

POLITICAL LIFE

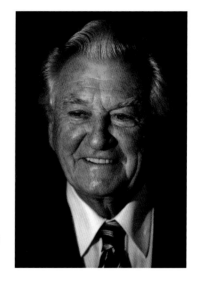

Hawke entered the House of Representative as a Labor minister in 1980. He became leader of the Labor Party in 1983 and one month later he led Labor to a landslide win, and was sworn in as prime minister.

During his first term, Hawke gained the highest popularity rating of any prime minister in history. He went on to lead Labor to victory at three more federal elections in 1984, 1987 and 1990.

During his time in office, Hawke made a number of reforms in the areas of education, the environment, workplace relations and the economy.

Paul Keating replaced Hawke as leader of the Labor Party in 1991. Hawke resigned from parliament in February 1992.

NOTABLE HONOURS & AWARDS

Companion of the Order of Australia (1979)

Freedom of the City of London (1999)

> **❝ Do you know why I have credibility? Because I don't exude morality. ❞**
>
> *– Bob Hawke*

Paul Keating
(1944–)

EARLY YEARS

Labor politician Paul Keating was born in Bankstown, New South Wales. After leaving school at the age of 15, he joined the Labor Party as soon as he could. He entered parliament in 1969 and, at only 25 years of age, was one of the youngest federal parliamentarians.

POLITICAL LIFE

Keating served as Treasurer under Prime Minister Bob Hawke from 1983 to 1991 and was responsible for a complete makeover of Australia's financial system and economy. Keating pushed for the Australian dollar to be floated on the open market, rather than set at a rate fixed to other major world currencies. From 1983 Keating encouraged foreign banks to operate in Australia to make the banking system more competitive.

In 1991 Bob Hawke resigned as leader of the Labor Party and Keating took over as Prime Minister of Australia.

THE 1993 ELECTION

Most people thought Labor could not win the 1993 election, as the party had already been in power for many years and the nation seemed ready for change. However, Keating won in a surprise victory after delivering a passionate speech to the nation and running a strong campaign that focused on creating jobs and reducing unemployment.

As prime minister, Keating was passionate about a number of issues. In particular, he felt strongly that Indigenous rights should be honoured and that it should be stated in writing that the continent of Australia was taken by force from its Indigenous inhabitants. He also felt Australia should become a republic and set up a committee to debate the possibility of Australia becoming independent from England.

Labor lost the 1996 federal election and Paul Keating resigned from parliament that same year.

Bob Brown
(1944–)

KEY ACHIEVEMENT
Leader of the
Australian Greens
from 1992 until 2012

EARLY YEARS

Politician, doctor and environmentalist Bob Brown was born in Oberon, New South Wales. He studied medicine at Sydney University, before working and studying overseas. He moved to Tasmania in 1972 and soon became involved in the environmental movement, joining the campaign to save Lake Pedder from being flooded. In March 1972, Brown became one of the founding members of the United Tasmania Group, Australia's first 'green party'.

POLITICAL LIFE

In 1978 Brown was appointed director of the Tasmanian Wilderness Society and was at the forefront of the campaign to stop the Franklin Dam from being built in Tasmania. In 1983 he was elected as the first Green member of the Tasmanian Parliament. Later that year, the federal government intervened to stop construction of the Franklin Dam.

During his time in state politics, Brown campaigned for a number of reforms around the issues of freedom of information, euthanasia, lowering parliamentary salaries, gay law reform, banning the battery-hen industry and making Tasmania nuclear-free. Brown resigned from state politics in 1993 and became a federal senator for Tasmania in 1996. He used this opportunity to support green and human rights issues, and to speak out strongly against anti-war issues like Australian participation in the 2003 invasion of Iraq.

In 2005 Brown became the first federal parliamentary leader of the Australian Greens. He was re-elected in 2007 and continued to support environmental issues by challenging then Prime Minister Kevin Rudd to set fixed carbon-emissions targets.

In 2012 Brown resigned as leader of the Greens and parliament. After retiring from parliament, he set up the Bob Brown Foundation and in 2013 he became leader of the Sea Shepherd Conservation Society, an organisation that works to conserve the sea and its marine life, particularly whales.

John Howard
(1939–)

EARLY YEARS

Former Liberal Prime Minister John Howard was born in Earlwood, New South Wales. He studied law at the University of Sydney.

POLITICAL LIFE

Howard entered parliament as the member for Bennelong in Sydney in 1974. He became a minister in the Coalition government under Malcolm Fraser after the dismissal of the Whitlam government in 1975. Howard later became Treasurer from 1977 until 1983, when the Fraser government lost the election.

Howard was leader of the Opposition from 1985 to 1989 and again in 1995. He became prime minister following the Liberal–National Party's victory in the 1996 federal election. As prime minister, Howard made a number of sweeping changes, such as selling Telstra, Australia's main phone and cable network, and introducing a goods and services tax (GST).

The Howard government also helped East Timor reach independence and took an active role in engaging with Asian countries as our nearest neighbours.

NOTABLE HONOURS & AWARDS

Companion of the Order of Australia (2008)

Presidential Medal of Freedom (2009)

Centenary Medal (2001)

Member of the Order of Merit (2012)

WAR AGAINST TERROR

A series of terrorist attacks on the United States in September 2001 brought the Australian and American governments closer together in terms of defence policy. The September 2001 attacks, along with the Bali bombings in 2002 when many Australian were killed, led Howard to declare a 'War Against Terror' and to commit Australian troops to wars in Afghanistan and Iraq. In the 2007 federal election, the Howard government suffered a landslide defeat and Howard lost his own seat. He retired from parliament the following year but remains active in public affairs.

Julia Gillard
(1961–)

KEY ACHIEVEMENT
First female Prime
Minister of Australia

EARLY YEARS

Former Labor Prime Minister Julia Gillard was born in Barry, Wales, and immigrated to Adelaide with her family in 1966. She studied arts/law at the University of Adelaide and at the University of Melbourne. After graduating, she worked as a solicitor in a law firm before being made partner in 1990.

POLITICAL LIFE

In 1998 Gillard successfully campaigned as the Labor candidate for the federal seat of Lalor in Victoria. In 2001 she was elected to the shadow cabinet, where she was given responsibility for Population and Immigration, and later Reconciliation and Indigenous Affairs, and Health.

In 2006, Kevin Rudd was elected leader of the Opposition, appointing Gillard as his deputy. When Labor won the 2007 federal election, she became the first female Deputy Prime Minister of Australia. But by June 2010, Rudd had lost the support of his party and Gillard successfully challenged him for the leadership role. She was elected as leader of the Labor Party and Prime Minister of Australia.

The 2010 federal election was a cliffhanger. Gillard's Labor government would have lost if not for the support received from a Green member of parliament (MP) and three Independent MPs, who voted with the government to form the first hung parliament since the 1940 federal election.

FIRST FEMALE PRIME MINISTER

The Gillard government introduced a carbon tax on large mining companies through the Clean Energy Bill, and also introduced reforms in the areas of health, education and immigration.

In June 2013 Kevin Rudd challenged Julia Gillard for the leadership of the Labor Party. Rudd won the leadership ballot, and Gillard resigned from her position as leader of the Labor party and Prime Minister of Australia.

Kevin Rudd
(1957–)

EARLY YEARS

Labor Prime Minister Kevin Rudd was born in Nambour, Queensland. He joined the Australian Labor Party in 1972, at the age of 15. After school he majored in Chinese Language and Chinese History at the Australian National University in Canberra.

POLITICAL LIFE

Rudd entered parliament in 1998 as a diplomat, a government official in Queensland and a consultant helping Australian firms do business in China. In 2001 he was appointed Shadow Minister for Foreign Affairs, taking on responsibility for International Security in 2003 and Trade in 2005. In 2006 Rudd was elected as leader of the Labor Party and spent the next year campaigning on issues of education reform, climate change, health care and fairness in Australian industrial relations laws. In 2007 Rudd became the second Queenslander in Australian history to lead his party to a federal election victory.

As prime minister from 2007 to 2010, Rudd signed the Kyoto Protocol on climate change, made a landmark apology to Indigenous Australians for the Stolen Generations, scrapped the unpopular WorkChoices Act (regarding rights in the workplace) and provided money to help working Australians cope with the global financial crisis.

One of the first things Rudd did as prime minister was deliver a Parliamentary Apology to Indigenous Australians for the Stolen Generations, officially acknowledging the injustice inflicted on Indigenous children who were forcibly removed from their families as part of a government policy that lasted from the early 1900s to the 1970s.

In 2010 Rudd resigned from his position as prime minister after his deputy, Julia Gillard, successfully challenged him for the leadership. After his resignation, he retained his seat at the 2010 federal election and Gillard appointed him Minister for Foreign Affairs. But after he challenged her for the leadership in February 2012 and lost, he resigned from that role and became a Labor backbencher, remaining in parliament but without a senior role.

28TH PRIME MINISTER OF AUSTRALIA

In June 2013 Rudd again challenged Julia Gillard for leadership of the Labor Party. Rudd won the challenge and was sworn in as the 28th Prime Minister of Australia on 27 June 2013.

> **"The Apology opened the opportunity for a new relationship based on mutual respect and mutual responsibility between Indigenous and non-Indigenous Australia. Because without mutual respect and mutual responsibility, the truth is we can achieve very little."**
>
> *– Prime Minister Kevin Rudd*

HAROLD HOLT *was the first prime minister in Australian history to hire a speech writer.*

John Howard's middle name is **'WINSTON'**, after British Prime Minister Winston Churchill.

Thanks to his university majors in Chinese Language and Chinese History, **KEVIN RUDD** is fluent in Mandarin. His name in Chinese is Lù Kèwén.

JOHN CURTIN is the only prime minister to have a gaol record after he protested against war conscription in 1916.

BILLY HUGHES WAS THROWN OUT OF THREE PARTIES AND REPRESENTED FOUR ELECTORATES IN TWO STATES DURING HIS TIME IN POLITICS.

In parliament, **GOUGH WHITLAM** was nicknamed 'the young brolga' due to his great height and, according to colleagues, his domineering nature.

Malcolm Fraser

was a strong supporter of black African movements. He was chosen to be part of an international group of 'eminent persons' charged with the task of ending apartheid in South Africa.

In 1997 refused to accept an appointment as a **Companion of the Order of Australia**, an honour offered to all past prime ministers since 1975.

BOB HAWKE holds honorary doctorates from universities in Australia and all over the world.

Aboriginal rights activist **NEVILLE BONNER** was passionate about boomerangs – one of his favourites was put on display at the Old Parliament House in Canberra.

"The motivations of a scientist are always mixed and complex . . . every medical student has the desire to do good in the world. Making a small contribution to that effort is really, in a sense, the last significant thing that I want to do in my life."

– Gustav Nossal

SCIENCE AND MEDICINE

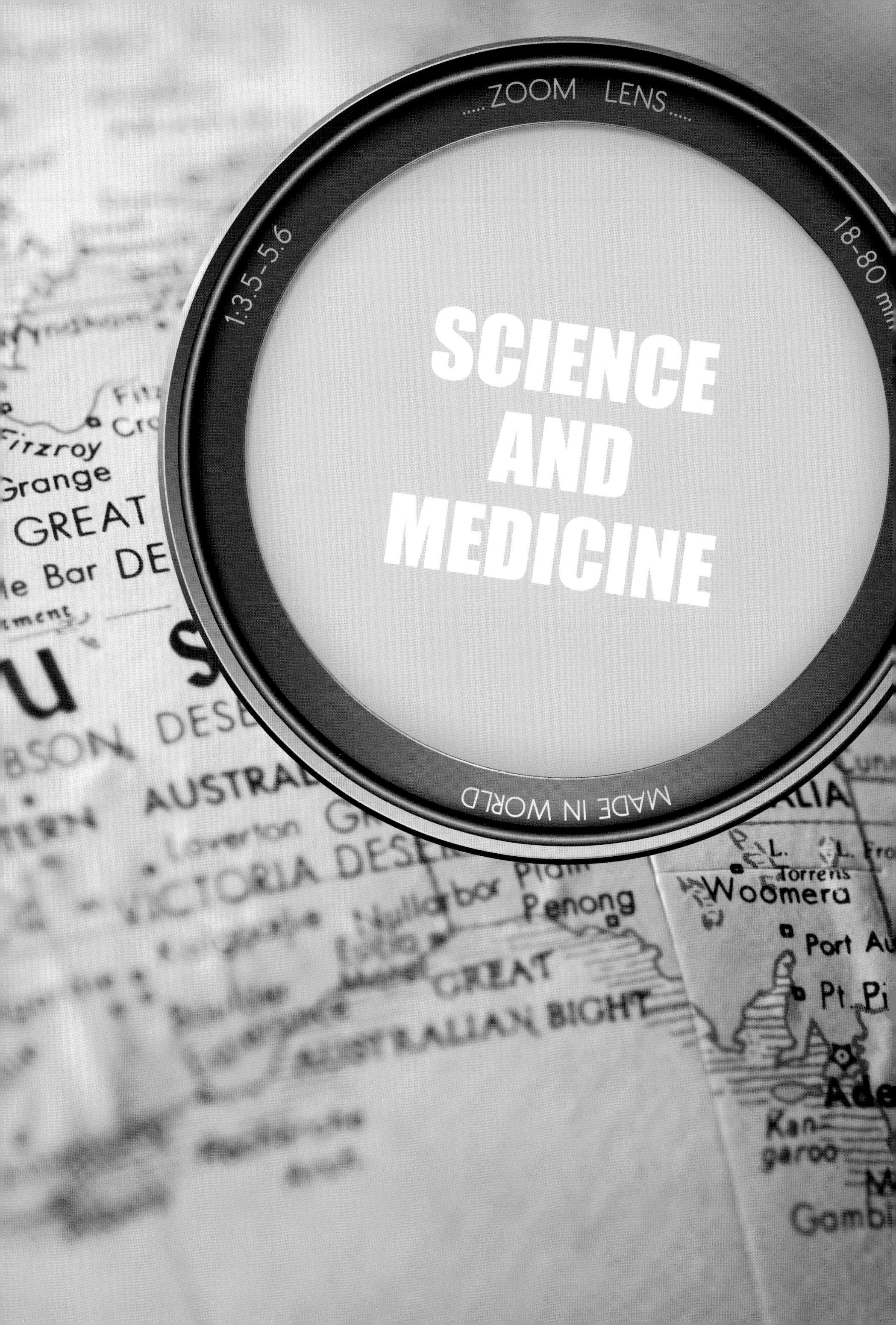

KEY ACHIEVEMENT
Discovered the use of penicillin as a way to fight bacteria

Howard Florey
(1898–1968)

EARLY YEARS

Medical scientist Howard Florey was born in Malvern, South Australia. He studied medicine at the University of Adelaide before going to England to complete his postgraduate studies at Oxford University and the University of Cambridge.

DISCOVERY OF PENICILLIN

In 1935 Florey was appointed Professor of Pathology at Oxford University and led a team of researchers looking into natural antibacterial substances. They soon discovered that penicillin mould had strong antibacterial effects on mice.

In 1941 Florey and his team treated their first human patient, who was suffering from infected wounds. Within a day of being given a small amount of penicillin, the patient began recovering, but the researchers did not have enough penicillin to administer and he died as a result.

Florey and his research team wanted to extract enough mould to produce penicillin commercially and they achieved this by 1945, just in time to provide the antibiotic to the Allies in the Second World War.

As a result of his work developing penicillin, Florey was awarded the 1945 Nobel Prize in Physiology or Medicine.

NOTABLE HONOURS & AWARDS

Fellow of the Royal Society (1941)

Knight Bachelor (1944)

Nobel Prize in Physiology or Medicine (1945)

Member of the Order of Merit (1965)

Life Peer (1965) and was created Baron Florey

❝ The worst part of being a doctor was the appalling thing of seeing young people maimed or wiped out, while one can do nothing. ❞

– Howard Florey

Frank Macfarlane Burnet
(1899–1985)

KEY ACHIEVEMENT
Won the 1960 Nobel Prize for Physiology or Medicine

EARLY YEARS

Medical scientist Frank Macfarlane Burnet was born in Traralgon, Victoria. In 1917 he won a scholarship to study Medicine at the University of Melbourne. He graduated in 1923 and became a senior resident in pathology at Melbourne's Walter and Eliza Hall Institute for Research in Pathology and Medicine. After spending a year in London conducting medical research, Burnet was appointed assistant director of the Hall Institute in 1928.

In 1932 Burnet was granted a two-year fellowship by the Institute of Medical Research in London to conduct research into viruses. Burnet returned to Australia in 1934 and spent the rest of his career researching viruses. He made a number of groundbreaking discoveries in the field, including finding the causes of Q fever, detecting the presence of the influenza virus and pinpointing what type or strain it is, and proving that humans cannot catch the myxomatosis disease from rabbits. Today's methods for producing influenza vaccines are still based on Burnet's work.

NOBEL PRIZE

In 1957 Burnet developed a particular interest in the field of immunology and the response of the human immune system to infection. He developed a theory about the impact of foreign substances on an under-developed immune system, which won him the Nobel Prize for Physiology or Medicine in 1960.

**NOTABLE
HONOURS & AWARDS**

Member of the Order
of Merit (1958)

Nobel Prize for Physiology
or Medicine (1960)

Australian of the Year (1960)

Knight Commander of the
Order of the British Empire
(1969)

Knight of the Order
of Australia (1978)

Edward 'Weary' Dunlop
(1907–1993)

EARLY YEARS

Surgeon Edward 'Weary' Dunlop was born in Wangaratta, Victoria. At the age of 16 he began an apprenticeship with a local pharmacist and three years later moved to Melbourne to attend Pharmacy College. Dunlop graduated at the top of his class and won a scholarship to study medicine at the University of Melbourne. It was here he was given the nickname 'Weary', which was a reference to his last name of Dunlop, which was also the name of a popular brand of tyres.

As well as being an excellent student, Dunlop was a champion sportsman and represented Australia in rugby in 1932.

Dunlop graduated from university in 1934 with first-class honours, and in 1935 he was offered a junior residency at Royal Melbourne Hospital. He also enlisted in the army at this time and was appointed to the Australian Army Medical Corps with the rank of Captain.

In 1938 Dunlop left Australia for London, where he did further training and was made a Fellow of the Royal College of Surgeons.

SECOND WORLD WAR

At the start of the Second World War in 1939, Dunlop again enlisted in the Australian Army Medical Corps. He was posted to the Middle East, where he developed a mobile surgical unit that could move around to treat wounded soldiers. He also served in Crete and Greece, and fought in the Battle of Tobruk.

In 1942 Dunlop was sent to Java in Indonesia to treat wounded allied soldiers. Three months later, he was captured by the Japanese and became a prisoner of war (POW). Dunlop was sent with other POWs to Thailand, where they were put to work building the Thailand–Burma Railway (also known as the Death Railway) between Bangkok and Rangoon. His medical skills, compassion and incredible courage in standing up to the Japanese inspired his fellow POWs to keep going.

After the war, Dunlop continued his distinguished medical career and became an ambassador for building bridges between Australia and Asia. His legacy as a brave leader during the Second World War continues to inspire modern-day Australians.

> **"Every country needs its heroes, and we must follow them."**
>
> *– Edward 'Weary' Dunlop*

John Tebbutt

BORN ▪ 1834 DIED ▪ 1916

Astronomer John Tebbutt was the first president of the Australian branch of the British Astronomical Association. He believed in sharing his scientific knowledge as widely as possible. In 1861 Tebbutt discovered 'The Great Comet', which remains one of the most brilliant known comets. Twenty years later he found another great comet. He wrote more than 350 articles about astronomy in scientific magazines.

Frank Fenner
(1914–2010)

KEY ACHIEVEMENT
Helped to eradicate the smallpox virus, and used the Myxoma virus to control Australia's rabbit epidemic

EARLY YEARS

Microbiologist and virologist Frank Fenner was born in Ballarat, Victoria. He studied medicine at the University of Adelaide, graduating in 1938 with Bachelor of Medicine and Bachelor of Surgery degrees, and as a Doctor of Medicine in 1942. He also graduated from the University of Sydney in 1940 with a Diploma of Tropical Medicine.

Fenner joined the Australian Army Medical Corps at the start of the Second World War. In 1942 he was posted to the Middle East, where he worked in the field ambulance. While he was in the Middle East, Fenner met Saul Adler, a famous parasitologist (a scientist who studies parasites). Through Adler, Fenner became interested in malaria, which was a problem disease in the Middle East and had become an epidemic in Asia. Fenner returned to Australia and spent the last two years of the war as a malariologist (a scientist specialising in the research of malaria), fighting to rid Papua New Guinea of malaria. In 1945 he was awarded an Order of the British Empire for this work.

NOTABLE HONOURS & AWARDS

Member of the Order of the British Empire (1945)

Companion of the Order of St Michael and St John (1976)

The Japan Prize for Preventative Medicine (1988)

Companion of the Order of Australia (1989)

Fellow of the Royal Society (1995)

Albert Einstein World Award of Science (2000)

ERADICATION OF THE SMALLPOX VIRUS

After the war, Fenner was invited to work alongside the eminent medical scientist Frank Macfarlane Burnet at the Walter and Eliza Hall Institute of Medical Research in Melbourne. Fenner's task was to eradicate the human smallpox virus. He was to do this by studying mousepox – a pox disease found in mice – to see if there were any similarities to the human smallpox virus. The papers he produced on this topic are still used today.

Fenner again turned his attention to the smallpox virus in 1977, when he was appointed chairman of the Global Commission for the Certification of Smallpox Eradication. At a World Health Organisation Assembly in 1980, Fenner

announced the worldwide eradication of the disease.
This was a huge achievement because smallpox had been
responsible for millions of deaths around the world.

MYXOMA VIRUS

In 1949 Fenner became Professor of Microbiology at the John
Curtin School of Medical Research in Canberra. At the time,
Australian farmers were struggling with rabbit plagues and
Fenner found that the myxoma virus was lethal to rabbits
and could be used as a way to control their numbers. It was
another important scientific breakthrough that changed the
lives of many Australians.

> **❝It was a terrific thrill to be involved in a
> program that in 10 years removed from the
> Earth a disease which, at the time we started,
> was credited with 20 million cases and two
> million deaths every year.❞**
>
> *– Frank Fenner on his work on malaria*

Dorothy Hill

BORN ▪ 1907   DIED ▪ 1997

Geologist Dorothy Hill was committed to science and to
raising academic standards at Australian universities. Hill
was the first female professor at an Australian university,
as well as the first female president of the Australian
Academy of Science.

Hill was born and raised in Brisbane, Queensland. She graduated from the
University of Queensland in 1928 with a First Class Honours degree in Geology, and a
Gold Medal for Outstanding Merit.

Vivian Bullwinkel
(1915–2000)

EARLY YEARS

Nurse Vivian Bullwinkel was born in Kapunda, South Australia. She trained as a nurse and midwife in Broken Hill before moving to Hamilton in Victoria to begin her nursing career at Kia-Ora Hospital. After the outbreak of the Second World War in 1939, Bullwinkel moved to Melbourne to enlist in the Australian Army.

BANKA ISLAND MASSACRE

In May 1941, Bullwinkel joined the Australian Army Nursing Service and was deployed to work in Singapore at the 2/13th Australian General Hospital. In February 1942, Singapore was invaded by Japanese troops and Bullwinkel, along with 65 fellow nurses, was forced to flee. They escaped on the SS *Vyner Brooke*, but the ship was sunk by Japanese forces only two days later. Bullwinkel plus a group of men, women, children and 22 of the nurses made it to shore on Banka Island. They were joined by a number of British soldiers from another sunk ship.

The group decided to surrender to the Japanese, but the men were killed anyway and the nurses were ordered to wade into the sea, where they were shot at from behind. Bullwinkel was struck by a bullet, but it went right through her body and she pretended to be dead until the Japanese soldiers left.

Bullwinkel was the only nurse who survived the massacre. She hid along with a wounded British soldier and nursed him, even though she was badly hurt herself. She was recaptured 12 days later and spent three-and-a-half years as a prisoner of war before the Japanese were defeated. Bullwinkel's account of the massacre was not made public until after the war.

Bullwinkel retired from the army in 1947 and devoted herself to nursing and to remembering the heroes killed on Banka Island.

NOTABLE
HONOURS & AWARDS

Florence Nightingale Medal

Royal Red Cross Medal (1947)

Efficiency Decoration (1969)

Member of the Most Excellent Order of the British Empire (1973)

Member of the Order of Australia (1993)

Fred Hollows
(1929–1993)

KEY ACHIEVEMENT
Restored eyesight to thousands of people around the world

EARLY YEARS

Ophthalmologist (eye doctor) Fred Hollows was born in Dunedin, New Zealand. He studied medicine at Otago Medical School before travelling to England to study ophthalmology at a leading eye hospital. After doing postgraduate study in Wales, Hollows moved to Australia in 1965 and was appointed Associate Professor of Ophthalmology at the University of New South Wales.

FIGHTING EYE DISEASE IN OUTBACK AUSTRALIA

During his time at the University of New South Wales, Hollows became aware that trachoma, an eye disease that can lead to blindness, was a big problem in Australia's remote and Aboriginal communities. Hollows knew the disease was preventable and campaigned the government to establish a national treatment program.

In 1975 the Australian government and the Australian College of Ophthalmologists set up the National Trachoma and Eye Health Program and appointed Hollows as chairman. The program was responsible for restoring eyesight to thousands of people around the country.

WORKING OVERSEAS

In the 1980s Hollows became a consultant for the World Health Organisation. He visited impoverished communities in Nepal, Eritrea and Vietnam, campaigning for improved health conditions and eye care to prevent widespread eye disease. He set up training programs for local people to perform eye surgery and laboratories to make and distribute cheap lenses for cataracts.

In 1992 Hollows established The Fred Hollows Foundation to provide eye care for poor and underprivileged people and to better the health of Indigenous Australians. One year later, Hollows died of cancer at the age of 63. The Fred Hollows Foundation continues the work he started.

NOTABLE HONOURS & AWARDS

Australian of the Year (1990)

Companion of the Order of Australia (1991)

Catherine Hamlin

BORN = 1924

Obstetrician and gynaecologist Catherine Hamlin co-founded Addis Ababa Fistula Hospital. The hospital is the only one in the world that offers free medical treatment and surgery to poor and disadvantaged women who have suffered injuries in childbirth. Hamlin has also pioneered new advances in the treatment of fistulas (an abnormality between two organs or vessels). She has been the recipient of numerous national and international humanitarian awards, including a Nobel Peace Prize nomination in 1999. Hamlin was made a Companion of the Order of Australia in 1995 and named a National Living Treasure in 2004.

Gustav Nossal

BORN = 1931

Medical researcher Gustav Nossal moved to Australia from Austria as a child. Nossal furthered the work of Frank Macfarlane Burnet to find out how the body builds immunity, protects itself against infections and builds up tolerance to transplants. As well as writing a number of books and articles about his research, Nossal was Chair of the committee overseeing the World Health Organisation's Vaccines and Biologicals Program from 1993 to 2002. He was also Chair of a committee of the Bill & Melinda Gates Foundation Children's Vaccine Program from 1998 to 2003.

Nossal has received many awards and tributes for his work. In 1970 he was appointed a Civil Commander of the Order of the British Empire for his contribution to medical research, and in 1977 the Queen knighted him for his groundbreaking work in immunology. Nossal became a Companion of the Order of Australia in 1989 for his service to medicine, science and the community. In 1997 he was listed as a National Living Treasure and was named Australian of the Year in 2000.

Graeme Clark
(1935–)

KEY ACHIEVEMENT
Invented the cochlear implant

EARLY YEARS

Professor Graeme Clark was born in Camden, New South Wales. His father, a pharmacist, was hearing impaired and Clark decided from a young age that he wanted to help people with hearing difficulties. Clarke studied medicine at the University of Sydney, graduating with honours in 1957.

In 1962 Clark moved to England, where he was senior surgeon at the Royal Ear, Nose and Throat Hospital, and then senior registrar in otolaryngology (the study of diseases relating to the ear and throat) at Bristol General Hospital. Clark decided to return to university in Australia in 1966 to do further study into treatments for profound deafness. This was the beginning of his research into cochlear implants.

COCHLEAR IMPLANT

In 1969 Clark was appointed William Gibson Chair of Otolaryngology at the University of Melbourne. It was in this role that Clark developed and implanted the first multi-channel cochlear implant.

Clark thought the sounds needed for speech could be reproduced in deaf people if the auditory nerve was stimulated electrically with sound patterns and the damaged or underdeveloped ear was bypassed altogether. While on holiday at the beach, he used a seashell to replicate the human cochlear (the spiral-shaped hearing cavity of the inner ear) and grass blades (bendy at the tip and stiffer further down) to represent the electrodes used to carry electricity. As a result of his research, Clark and a colleague performed the first multi-channel cochlear implant operation at the Royal Victorian Eye and Ear Hospital in 1978. The implant enabled the recipient to recognise a range of different sound frequencies.

In 1983 Clark founded the Bionic Ear Institute 'to give deaf children and adults the opportunity to participate as fully as possible in the hearing world and to find new ways to restore brain function'.

**NOTABLE
HONOURS & AWARDS**
Officer of the Order
of Australia (1983)

KEY ACHIEVEMENT
Discovered new mammal species and helped raise national awareness about climate change

Tim Flannery
(1956–)

EARLY YEARS

Scientist, environmental activist and writer Tim Flannery was born in Melbourne, Victoria. He studied English literature at La Trobe University before switching to science for his postgraduate studies. Flannery completed a masters degree in Earth Science at Monash University in 1981 and a doctorate in Palaeontology (the study of fossils) at the University of New South Wales in 1985.

NEW MAMMAL SPECIES

As part of his doctoral studies, Flannery researched the evolution of kangaroos and related animals. In 1985 he took part in research that led to the discovery of Australian mammal fossils from the Cretaceous period. They were more than 80 million years older than any other previously discovered specimens.

From 1984 to 1999 Flannery was the principal research scientist in mammalogy (the study of mammals) at the Australian Museum in Sydney. During this time, he went on a number of expeditions to Papua New Guinea and discovered 16 species and subspecies of mammals, including four kangaroo species.

NOTABLE HONOURS & AWARDS

Australian of the Year
(2007)

ENVIRONMENTAL ACTIVISM

In 1994 Flannery released his book *The Future Eaters: An Ecological History of Australasian Lands and People*, in which he argued that Australia's natural resources are limited and we are not leaving enough for the future. The book was a bestseller and Flannery has become a leading spokesperson and activist for environmental change.

In his 2005 book *The Weather Makers*, Flannery explained the science behind climate change and predicted that if we didn't reduce carbon emissions, governments would impose rules to make it happen.

In 2007 Flannery became Professor in the Climate Risk Concentration of Research Excellence at Macquarie University and in 2011 the Australian government appointed Flannery Chief Commissioner of the Climate Commission.

Simon Chapman

BORN ▪ 1951

Simon Chapman is an academic, researcher and public health policy advocate, specialising in the area of tobacco control. He has played a major role in reducing the smoking rate in Australia from 45 percent of men and 30 percent of women in 1978 to 15 percent in all adults today. Chapman was made an Officer of the Order of Australia in 2013 for distinguished service to medical research.

Ian Frazer

BORN ▪ 1953

Immunologist Ian Frazer, along with his colleague Jian Zhou, developed a vaccine that prevents infection with Human Papilloma Virus (HPV) and cervical cancer. Originally born in Scotland, Frazer moved to Australia in 1981 and is Chief Executive and Director of Research at the Translational Research Institute in Queensland. Frazer was named Australian of the Year in 2006 and won the Prime Minister's Prize for Science in 2008. He was made a Companion of the Order of Australia in 2012 and is a National Living Treasure.

"I guess it's no secret that this 21st century of ours is going to be the make-and-break century of sustainability."

– Tim Flannery

KEY ACHIEVEMENT
Pioneered modern heart transplant procedures

Victor Chang
(1936–1991)

EARLY YEARS

Heart surgeon Victor Chang was born in Shanghai, China. He grew up in Hong Kong before moving to Australia in 1953. Chang studied medicine at the University of Sydney and trained as a surgeon in England and the United States. He was awarded fellowships to the Royal College of Surgeons, the Australasian College of Surgeons and the American College of Surgeons. In 1972 Chang joined the cardiothoracic team at St Vincent's Hospital in Sydney.

HEART TRANSPLANT PROGRAM

In the early 1980s heart transplants became more feasible after the development of an anti-rejection drug. Chang recognised the need for an Australian heart transplant program and worked tirelessly lobbying the government and the business community for money to help finance a national program. As a result of Chang's work, the National Heart Transplant Program was established at St Vincent's Hospital in 1984.

That year, Chang operated on Australia's youngest heart transplant patient, a 14-year-old girl. He went on to perform more than 197 heart transplants and 14 heart–lung transplants before 1990. Chang also began research into the development of an artificial heart.

In 1991 Chang was murdered by two men attempting to rob him. The men were jailed for his murder and have since been released and deported to Malaysia.

NOTABLE HONOURS & AWARDS

Companion of the Order of Australia (1986)

Australian of the Century at the People's Choice Awards (1999)

❝I always get upset when I do this, because it means someone has to die so that someone else can live.❞

– Victor Chang on organ transplants

Charles Teo

(1957–)

KEY ACHIEVEMENT
Pioneered a new approach to the treatment of brain disorders and injuries

EARLY YEARS

Neurosurgeon Charles Teo was born in Mosman, New South Wales. He studied medicine and surgery at the University of New South Wales before spending ten years working in the United States, where he still teaches for part of the year.

TREATMENT OF BRAIN DISORDERS AND INJURIES

In 2001 Teo established the Cure for Life Foundation with the aim of raising funds and advancing research into a cure for brain cancer.

Teo returned to Australia in 2006 as Director of the Centre for Minimally Invasive Neurosurgery at the Prince of Wales Hospital in Sydney, and quickly developed a reputation for his unorthodox approach to brain surgery. Teo is known, and sometimes criticised, for performing radical brain surgeries on patients whom other doctors have deemed to be incurable. His methods, however, have saved or extended the lives of many patients both in Australia and overseas.

❝Trust is the most important thing. I have to trust my patients as much as they trust me. A patient has to understand that a doctor cares for them. Not that he's the smartest guy, but there is this trust that he will do the right thing by them.❞

– Charles Teo

NOTABLE HONOURS & AWARDS

Humanitarian Service Award by Rotary International (2008)

Member of the Order of Australia (2011)

KEY ACHIEVEMENT
Invented spray-on skin for burns victims to stop infection and scarring

Fiona Wood
(1958–)

EARLY YEARS

Plastic surgeon Fiona Wood was born in Yorkshire, England and studied medicine at St Thomas' Hospital in London. She married an Australian surgeon and immigrated to Perth in 1987, and became a registrar in plastic surgery at the Sir Charles Gardiner Hospital.

SPRAY-ON SKIN

In 1993 Wood began working with medical scientist Marie Stoner on a revolutionary new treatment for burns victims. This involved using a burns victim's own healthy skin cells to generate new cells, which were then sprayed over the burnt area. This process enabled the faster growth of skin tissue and lessened the scarring inflicted by skin grafts.

Wood and Stoner started a company called Clinical Cell Culture (C3), which has since been renamed Avita Medical, to produce cells for use by surgeons around the world. The money made from Avita Medical is used to fund further burns research.

In 2002 Wood led the Perth medical team that worked to save the lives of 28 burns victims who were flown to Australia after the Bali bombings, which killed 202 people, including 88 Australians. She became famous for her compassion at the time of the crisis and for her success rate in the treatment of the Bali burns victims.

Awards 2005

NOTABLE HONOURS & AWARDS

Member of the Order of Australia (2003)

National Living Treasure (2004)

Australian Citizen of the Year (2004)

Australian of the Year (2005)

Brian Schmidt

BORN ▪ 1967

Astrophysicist Brian Schmidt won the 2011 Nobel Prize for physics for his research proving that the expansion of the universe is accelerating. Born in the United States, Schmidt moved to Australia in 1994 and is now a Research Fellow at the Mount Stromlo and Siding Spring Observatories. He is also a Fellow of the Royal Society.

Terence Tao

BIRTH ▪ 1975

Award-winning mathematician Terence Tao was doing university-level maths courses by the time he was nine. From 1986 to 1988 he was the youngest person to enter the International Mathematical Olympiad, where he won bronze, silver and gold medals. At 16 years of age, Tao graduated with bachelors and masters degrees from Flinders University in South Australia, and in 1992 he won a scholarship to study in the United States. By the time he was 24, Tao was the youngest person ever appointed a full professor at University of California, Los Angeles (UCLA). Tao is particularly known for his mathematical theorems, which include the Green–Tao theorem, Tao's inequality, the Kakeya conjecture and the Horn conjecture. Tao won the Australian Mathematical Society Medal in 2004 and 2006 and the Fields Medal in 2006, and became a Fellow of the Royal Society in 2007.

> **❝My overwhelming feeling at that time and subsequently has been one of feeling very privileged to have been able to have helped.❞**
>
> *– Fiona Wood on her work during the 2002 Bali bombings*

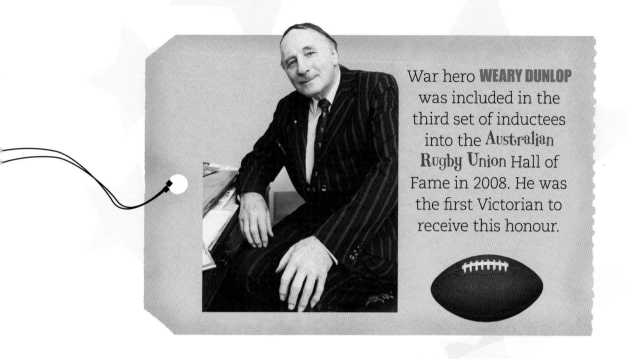

War hero **WEARY DUNLOP** was included in the third set of inductees into the Australian Rugby Union Hall of Fame in 2008. He was the first Victorian to receive this honour.

Australian Nobel Prize Winners

NAME	YEAR	CATEGORY	ACHIEVEMENT
Brian Schmidt	2011	Physics	Discovery of the accelerating universe theory
Elizabeth Blackburn	2009	Physiology or Medicine	Work on telemeres and the enzyme telemorase in chemistry and genetics
Barry Marshall and Robin Warren	2005	Physiology or Medicine	Discovery of the bacterium *Helicobacter pylori* in gastritis and peptic ulcer disease
Peter Doherty	1996	Physiology or Medicine	Discoveries on the cell mediated immune system
John Cornforth	1975	Physiology or Medicine	Advance in knowledge of enzymes
Bernard Katz	1970	Physiology or Medicine	Discoveries in nerve biochemistry
John Carew Eccles	1963	Physiology or Medicine	Discoveries relating to nerve cells
Frank Macfarlane Burnet	1960	Physiology or Medicine	Advance in knowledge of the immunological system
Howard Florey	1945	Physiology or Medicine	Discovery of penicillin
William Henry Bragg and William Lawrence Bragg	1915	Physics	Advance in knowledge of crystal structure analysis and X-rays

In 2007 **DR FIONA WOOD** was invited to travel to Indonesia after the crash landing of Garuda Indonesia Flight 200, to help care for burns victims.

A life-size bronze statue of heart surgeon **VICTOR CHANG** stands outside the Victor Chang Cardiac Research Institute in Sydney.

Scientist and environmentalist **Tim Flannery** has a species of bat named after him: the **Greater Monkey-faced Bat** (Pteralopex flanneryi).

of the Year Awards 2005

"Architecture is not an inspirational business, it's a rational procedure to do sensible and hopefully beautiful things; that's all."

– Harry Seidler

ARCHITECTURE AND DESIGN

Francis Greenway

BORN ▪ 1777   DIED ▪ 1837

English-born architect Francis Greenway was transported to New South Wales for the crime of forgery. Between 1816 and 1818, while still a convict, Greenway designed and constructed the Macquarie Lighthouse on South Head, at the entrance to Port Jackson in Sydney. Because the project was so successful, he was given his freedom by Governor Lachlan Macquarie and became Australia's first government architect. He built many of the most important buildings in the new colony, including St Matthew's Church in Windsor, and Sydney's St James' Church and Hyde Park Barracks.

Edmund Blacket

BORN ▪ 1817   DIED ▪ 1883

Architect Edmund Blacket's Gothic design-style helped shape the look of a number of Sydney buildings, particularly churches and cathedrals. Blacket was born in England and arrived in Sydney in 1842. His work was embraced by the Church of England in New South Wales and Blacket became their favourite architect, designing three cathedrals and more than fifty parish churches during his career. From 1849 to 1854, he held the prestigious role of official Colonial Architect to New South Wales and designed many public buildings, including the University of Sydney, St Andrew's Cathedral, and St Saviour's Cathedral in Goulburn. These edifices are known for their tall grand designs, flying buttresses spanning the outside walls, pointed arches, vaulted ceilings, light and airy inside spaces, and use of gargoyles and other decorations.

Walter Burley Griffin
(1876–1937)

KEY ACHIEVEMENT
Won the international competition to design Australia's capital city, Canberra

EARLY YEARS

American-born architect Walter Burley Griffin came to Australia in 1913 with his wife, Marion Griffin, after Walter won an international competition to design Australia's new capital city, Canberra.

DESIGNING CANBERRA

In April 1911 the Australian government held an international competition to design its new capital city, Canberra. The Griffins found out about the competition while they were on their honeymoon and Walter came up with a design, which Marion then drew up in great detail. In 1912 Walter's design won and the couple travelled to Australia to look at the site of the new city. While in Australia, Walter got the job of Federal Capital Director of Design and Construction and was able to oversee the design of North and South Canberra. With the outbreak of the First World War in 1914, however, money became limited and the plans for Canberra had to change. Walter resigned from the project in 1920.

Although Burley Griffin was not properly appreciated for his Canberra design in his lifetime, in 1964 Prime Minister Robert Menzies insisted that Canberra's central lake be named Lake Burley Griffin in Walter's honour.

The Griffins decided to remain in Australia and took on a number of projects in Melbourne, such as the Capitol Theatre. In 1919 the couple founded the Greater Sydney Development Association (GSDA) and bought 259 hectares of land in North Sydney to develop a well-designed community of homes set in bushland. The community is today known as the suburb of Castlecrag.

Canberra's city landscape

"Australia, of most democratic tendencies and bold radical government, may well be expected to look upon her great future, and with it her federal capital, with characteristic big vision."

– Walter Burley Griffin

John Bradfield

BORN ▪ 1867   DIED ▪ 1943

Engineer John Bradfield was best known for overseeing the design and construction of the Sydney Harbour Bridge. In addition, Bradfield was Chief Engineer of Sydney's metropolitan railway construction. In 1915 he came up with a master plan for the city's railways: suburban railways would be made electric, a city underground railway would be built and the Sydney Harbour Bridge would carry the tracks over the harbour. The Bradfield Highway, the main roadway section of the Harbour Bridge, is named in his honour. Bradfield was also the designer and consulting engineer for Brisbane's Story Bridge and for the Cataract Dam in Sydney and Burrinjuck Dam in Yass. He also designed the Circular Quay railway station in Sydney, although it was built after his death.

Roy Grounds

BORN ▪ 1905   DIED ▪ 1981

Roy Grounds was one of the pioneers of the modernist architectural movement in Australia and was known for designing buildings that were in harmony with their environment. Later in his career, he began incorporating strong geometric shapes into his buildings, such as the triangular Leyser House at Kew, Victoria. One of Grounds' most famous buildings is the Melbourne National Art Gallery and Cultural Centre. Grounds received a knighthood from the Queen in 1969 for his services to architecture.

Robin Boyd
(1919–1971)

KEY ACHIEVEMENT
Pioneered a modern, international style for Australian homes in the 1950s and 1960s

EARLY YEARS

Architect Robin Boyd was born in Armadale, Victoria. He studied architecture at Melbourne University and Melbourne Technical College. While Boyd was at university, Boyd formed the Victorian Architectural Students' Society and founded the newspaper *Smudges*, where he expressed his radical ideas about modern architecture.

In 1940 Boyd won the position of sole assistant to leading modernist architect Roy Grounds. Boyd served in the Australian Army during the Second World War, but maintained his interest in architecture throughout that time.

WELL-DESIGNED, INEXPENSIVE HOUSES

In 1946 Boyd became the first director of the Small Homes Service, which was part of the Royal Victorian Institute of Architects.

Boyd first came to public attention in the late 1940s, when he became known for his passionate views about modern well-designed houses that were also cheap, functional and partially prefabricated for easy construction. He used his position as Director of the Small Homes Service to ensure the housing was accessible and affordable for the 'average' Australian.

In 1953 Boyd joined with his former mentor Roy Grounds and Frederick Romberg to form a dynamic Melbourne architectural firm, which became a driving force in Australian architecture through the 1950s and 1960s.

NOTABLE HONOURS & AWARDS
Commander of the Order of the British Empire (1971)

❝ We need better architecture and planning: more imaginatively exciting, more involving, more our own. ❞

– *Robin Boyd*

Harry Seidler
(1923–2006)

EARLY YEARS

Architect Harry Seidler was born in Vienna, Austria. He escaped the 1938 Nazi invasion of Austria by fleeing to England as a teenager. Seidler studied building and construction at Cambridge Technical College. In 1940, he was arrested as an enemy alien and sent to a prison camp in Canada. When he was released 18 months later he resumed his architectural training, this time at the University of Manitoba. After graduating, Seidler won a scholarship to the Harvard School of Design in the United States. There, Seidler studied under Walter Gropius, the founder of the revolutionary Bauhaus School of modernist design. This period was to have a huge influence on Seidler's own modernist architectural style. In the late 1940s both Seidler and his parents immigrated to Sydney. Seidler's parents asked him to design their home. The mainly timber building, known as the Rose Seidler House, is named after his mother and remains one of Seidler's most domestic residences.

Australia Square

ARCHITECTURE

Seidler's work transformed Sydney's city skyline. In the 1960s his Australia Square project (1961 to 1967) was the world's tallest lightweight concrete building. HIs radical design used circular office towers for the first time, with large open spaces for office workers and passersby.

In the 1990s, Seidler used advances in technology to incorporate concrete curves and curved roofs into his Horizon apartment tower, which was completed in 1998. He introduced curved verandahs into the building, which is 143.9 metres tall and includes 260 apartments.

Seidler designed approximately 180 buildings in his lifetime and his architect wife, Penelope Seidler, carried on his work when he died.

NOTABLE HONOURS & AWARDS

Companion of the Order of Australia (1987)

Officer of the Order of the British Empire (1992)

Glenn Murcutt

BORN ▪ 1936

Glenn Murcutt is one of Australia's most famous contemporary architects. In 2002 Murcutt won the prestigious Pritzker Prize (like the Nobel Prize for architects) and the American Institute of Architects Gold Medal in 2009. He is renowned for using corrugated iron in his work and is sometimes known as 'the tin man'. Murcutt's buildings include Marie Short House (1975), Fredericks House (1982), Ball-Eastaway House (1983), Magney House (1984), Marika-Alderton House (1994), and Arthur and Yvonne Boyd Education Centre (1999).

"The observations made by the Commissioner and others, upon the explanation of those plans, were I should make a city superior in architectural beauty to London . . . The Commissioner thought with them that I was too grand in my notions of building for this infant colony."

– Francis Greenway

Philip Cox
(1939–)

EARLY YEARS

Award-winning architect Philip Cox was born on Sydney's North Shore. He studied architecture at the University of Sydney and graduated with a Doctorate of Science from the University of New South Wales.

MEMORABLE BUILDINGS

In 1963 Cox established his first architectural partnership, and in 1967 he opened his own practice, Philip Cox and Associates.

Cox has designed many of Sydney's award-winning buildings, including the Sydney Olympic Stadium, the Sydney Exhibition Centre, the Australian National Maritime Museum at Darling Harbour, the Sydney Football Stadium, the Australian Broadcasting Corporation building and King Street Wharf. Cox also designed Melbourne's Flinders Park Tennis Centre, and Longitude 131 at Uluru in the Northern Territory.

NOTABLE HONOURS & AWARDS

Gold Medal by the Royal Australian Institute of Architects (1984)

Officer of the Order of Australia (1988)

Sydney Olympic Stadium railway station

Benjamin Dunkerley
(1839–1918)

EARLY YEARS

Hat designer and manufacturer Benjamin Dunkerley was born in Cheshire, England. He immigrated to Tasmania in 1874 and opened the Kensington Hat Factory in Hobart the following year.

In 1892 Dunkerley achieved international recognition when he invented a machine that revolutionised fur-hat making around the world. The machine removed the hair tip from rabbit fur, leaving the under-fur to be used for felt hats. This time-consuming process had previously been done by hand.

Dunkerley and his family moved from Tasmania to Victoria in 1895 and then to Sydney in the early 1900s. In Sydney, Dunkerley opened a small hat factory in Surry Hills to supply Australian hatters with rabbit fur and machinery.

THE AKUBRA HAT

In 1911 the hat factory became Dunkerley Hat Mills Ltd. The following year the factory moved to larger premises, to facilitate increased production of their popular slouch-style felt hats.

At the start of the First World War, Dunkerley Hat Mills was asked to produce slouch hats for the Australian Army, and the hats soon became an iconic part of the military uniform. It was at this time that the hats were given the brand name 'Akubra', which is believed to be an Aboriginal word for 'head covering.'

When Dunkerley died in 1918, ownership of the company was transferred to his son-in-law, Stephen Keir, who had previously been General Manager. The company started trading under the name Akubra. Akubra continues to be owned and run by several generations of the Keir family today.

KEY ACHIEVEMENT
Founded Australia's most iconic wallpaper-design company

Florence Broadhurst
(1899–1977)

EARLY YEARS

Designer and entrepreneur Florence Broadhurst was born in Mount Perry, Queensland. When she was 23, Broadhurst travelled to South East Asia and China as part of the musical comedy group the Globe Trotters. In 1926 Broadhurst opened the Broadhurst Academy in Shanghai, which taught a variety of musical instruments and singing, along with ballroom and classical dancing, and journalism.

Three years later, Broadhurst moved to England and set up a design business with her first husband. After living in the United Kingdom during the Second World War, Broadhurst returned to Australia with her second husband and son in 1949.

Broadhurst took up painting and produced a series of 114 landscape paintings in two years. Her work was critically well received and was exhibited in major galleries around Australia. She became a founding member of the Art Gallery Society of New South Wales and was a member of the Society of Interior Designers of Australia.

AUSTRALIAN HAND-PRINTED WALLPAPERS

In 1959 Broadhurst opened a design studio called Australian (Hand-Printed) Wallpapers Pty Ltd. Along with a small team of staff she produced innovative hand-crafted wallpaper in vivid styles with bright colours and large geometric patterns. She also developed a number of new design techniques, such as printing on metallic surfaces, coating the wallpaper with washable vinyl and drying paper on racks in large quantities. By 1972 Broadhurst had established her reputation both nationally and overseas with a library of 800 wallpaper designs in 80 different colours and styles.

In 1977 Broadhurst was found dead in her Paddington studio. Her employees and friends believed she was murdered by someone she may have known, as two cups of tea were found near her body. The mystery of her death is yet to be solved.

In 1978 Broadhurst's library of designs was sold. But because wallpaper went out of fashion, they were not used for some years until Signature Prints, the final owner, decided to market 530 of Broadhurst's designs at the beginning of the 2000s and promote them overseas. In 2008 a Sydney-based rug company launched its Florence Broadhurst Rug Collection.

Prue Acton

BORN ▪ 1943

Known as Australia's 'golden girl' of fashion in the 1960s, designer Prue Acton was born in Benalla, Victoria. She studied art with a major in textiles at the Royal Melbourne Institute of Technology, graduating in 1963. That same year, Acton started her own design business in Melbourne's Flinders Lane. Acton's clothes set the mood of the 1960s with her use of bold colours and modern new fabrics. In 1967 Acton achieved international success when she became the first female Australian designer to have a fashion show in

Expo uniforms designed by Prue Acton in 1974

New York. Acton designed Australian uniforms for events such as the 1974 Expo and the 1978, 1984 and 1988 Olympic Games. She was appointed Officer of the Order of the British Empire in 1982, and has won many fashion awards throughout her career.

❝As the Australians' taste in décor was generally conservative, I realised that it would not be an easy task to persuade them to be a little more adventurous with the effects of bold colour and colour harmony, and in addition to try the effects of three dimensions and colour vibration as well as using metal papers.❞

– Florence Broadhurst

George Bond

BORN ▪ 1876 DIED ▪ 1950

Founder of the Bonds clothing brand George Bond was born in Kentucky, America. He immigrated to Sydney in 1906 and ten years later set up his own business selling imported stockings and underwear. During the First World War, Bond started making his own garments. There was a shortage of materials from overseas, so Bond set up a factory for spinning and weaving cotton to make underwear. By 1927, as the managing director of George A. Bond & Co. Ltd, Bond was employing 2,600 people. He also owned two cotton farms and produced about one-quarter of Australia's cotton and knitted goods. The Bond brand was famous for its 'Chesty Bonds' singlet, which remains an iconic item of Australian clothing. In the late 1920s, Bond was unable to pay back the large amounts of money he had borrowed from the bank. The company was sold in 1930 to a group called Bonds Industries Ltd, who continue to run it today.

Reginald Murray Williams

BORN ▪ 1908 DIED ▪ 2003

Bushman and entrepreneur Reginald Murray Williams founded the iconic R.M. Williams outback clothing company, best known for their handcrafted riding boots. In 1985 Williams was appointed a Companion of the Order of St Michael and St George for services to the outback community. In 1992 he was named an Officer of the Order of Australia for service to business and to the community, and in 2001 he was awarded the Centenary Medal.

Jenny Kee

BORN ▪ 1947

Jenny Kee is a fashion designer whose brightly coloured jumpers, knitted from Australian wool and featuring native flowers and animals helped shape Australia's image abroad. Kee was born in Bondi to Chinese and European parents. In the late 1960s Kee formed a partnership with fashion and textile designer Linda Jackson, and together they created iconic knitted jumpers, which became popular worldwide. Kee's artworks have been exhibited at museums, such as the Art Gallery of NSW and the Australian National Gallery, and are sold overseas.

Collette Dinnigan

BORN ▪ 1965

South African-born Australian fashion designer Collette Dinnigan started her own clothing label in 1990 with a range of dry-clean only underwear. Dinnigan achieved international success in 1995, when she became the first Australian to launch a ready-to-wear collection in Paris. Her collections now include designs for lingerie, bridal wear and children's wear, all of which are exported internationally.

Reg Mombassa

MAMBO FOUNDED ▪ 1984

Artist Reg Mombassa is best known for his abstract designs for the surfwear company Mambo Graphics. Mombassa was born Christopher O'Doherty in New Zealand. In 1969 he immigrated to Sydney, where he studied art. As well as his his bright, bold cartoons for Mambo, he also paints landscapes and portraits, which can be seen in many of Australia's major art galleries.

Gordon and Rena Merchant

BILLABONG FOUNDED ▪ 1975

Founders of the Billabong surfwear company. The Merchants started designing and making boardshorts from their home at Burleigh Heads, Queensland, in 1973. Gordon designed the shorts using his now famous triple-stitching technique, which ensured greater durability. The Merchants called their label 'Billabong', which is a combination of the Wiradjuri words 'Billa', meaning river or creek, and 'bong', meaning to die. Together the words refer to a stagnant body of water attached to a waterway. Billabong's popularity grew, and in 1975 the Merchants opened their first factory and were soon exporting clothes and accessories overseas. The business expanded to include a number of other brands, and by the beginning of 2012 Billabong owned 677 stores worldwide. Later that year, however, trouble struck and Billabong had to downsize.

Tony and Mark Brown

KUTA LINES FOUNDED ▪ 1970s

Founded by brothers Tony and Mark Brown in the 1970s, the Kuta Lines clothing style is inspired by the traditional Indonesian art of ikat weaving and dying techniques, which Tony had encountered on a surfing trip to Bali. The brothers used a heavy cloth material to create a fleecy garment that keeps surfers cosy and warm, on and off the beach. Kuta Lines surfwear expanded globally during the 1980s and 1990s, and is now available in Malaysia, Spain and Mexico.

Marc Newson
(1963–)

KEY ACHIEVEMENT
Designed the iconic Lockheed Lounge chair and the Embryo chair

EARLY YEARS

Industrial designer Marc Newson was born in the northern suburbs of Sydney. He studied jewellery and sculpture at the Sydney College of the Arts.

LOCKHEED LOUNGE AND EMBRYO CHAIR

In 1986 Newson won a grant from the Crafts Board of the Australia Council, which allowed him to create the Lockheed Lounge, the first of what was to become a series of iconic furniture pieces made from unusual materials.

The Lockheed Lounge was Newson's first breakthrough piece of furniture. It is made from aluminium and fibreglass and has a sleek form, which is typical of Newson's designs. Similarly, his embryo chair, which was created in 1988, has a smooth, sculptural design and contributed to Newson's reputation as one of Australia's most influential industrial designers.

Embryo chair

OTHER DESIGNS

Newson has worked for some of the leading consumer design brands in the world. As well as furniture, he has designed clothing, jewellery, airport lounges and cars. His work appears in museums around the world.

NOTABLE HONOURS & AWARDS
Commander of the Order of the British Empire (2012)

❝I think it's really important to design things with a kind of personality.❞

– Marc Newson

ARTIST
REG MOMBASSA
formed the rock band Mental As Anything (or The Mentals) in 1976 with four art school friends. They went on to become one of Australia's most popular bands with a huge international following.

As well as being the first Australian to launch a ready-to-wear collection in Paris, fashion designer *Collette Dinnigan* was the first designer to be asked to appear in the parade herself.

As well as being a well-established wallpaper designer, *Florence Broadhurst* was also an accomplished banjolele player – it's a small ukulele with a banjo-like shape.

The iconic Akubra hat, invented by hatter BENJAMIN DUNKERLEY, has been worn by Australian Olympians in past OLYMPIC GAMES ceremonies.

Living in the Blue Mountains, fashion designer **JENNY KEE** often travelled to Sydney by train and in 1977 she and her daughter survived the horrific **Granville rail disaster** in which 83 people died.

Modernist architect **ROBIN BOYD** wrote nine books, including *Australia's Home* (the first history of Australian homes) in 1952, and *The Australian Ugliness* (a critique of tastes in architecture and popular culture) in 1960.

Marion Griffin was one of the world's first licensed female architects.

Award-winning designer **Marc Newson** was selected as one of *Time magazine's* 100 most influential people of the year in 2005.

In 1967 fashion designer **Prue Acton** launched her own range of makeup to match her clothes.

"Wherever you are in the world, there's always something about the Australian light. There's something about the sharpness of it, something about the clarity of it, something about the colours of Australia. And, hopefully, something optimistic about Australian painting too."

– Ken Done

FINE ARTS

William Dobell
(1899–1970)

EARLY YEARS

Painter William Dobell was born in Newcastle, New South Wales. After school he became an apprentice draughtsman at a local architecture firm, before moving to Sydney in 1923. The following year Dobell enrolled in art classes at the Julian Ashton Art School. In 1929 he was awarded the Society of Artists' travelling scholarship and went to England to study at the Slade School. Dobell spent ten years in Europe, living and painting in Belgium and Paris before returning to Australia in 1939.

PORTRAITURE

Back in Australia, Dobell rented an apartment in Kings Cross in Sydney and began painting vibrant portraits of local personalities, developing what has become known as a 'gallery of Australian characters'.

During the Second World War Dobell worked as a camouflage artist and then as an official war artist from 1942 to 1944. His paintings at this time continued to focus on people and personalities.

Dobell won the prestigious Archibald Prize three times: in 1943, for *Portrait of an Artist* depicting fellow artist Joshua Smith; in 1948, for a painting of his friend and fellow artist Margaret Olley (he also won the Wynne Prize that year for *Storm Approaching Wangi*); and in 1959, for his portrait of Dr EG MacMahon.

NOTABLE HONOURS & AWARDS

Archibald Prize (1943; 1948; 1959)

Wynne Prize (1948)

Officer of the Order of the British Empire (1965)

Knighthood (1966)

❝A sincere artist is not one who makes a faithful attempt to put on to canvas what is in front of him, but one who tries to create something which is, in itself, a living thing.❞

– William Dobell

Heidelberg School

The Heidelberg School was an important art movement originating in the late 1880s. The movement was named after Heidelberg in Victoria, where the artists associated with the movement spent much of their time painting and drawing inspiration from the bush landscape. Some of the main artists associated with Heidelberg include Frederick McCubbin, Tom Roberts, Arthur Streeton, Charles Condor, Walter Withers, Louis Abrahams and Jane Sutherland.

Frederick McCubbin BORN ▪ 1855   DIED ▪ 1917

McCubbin is most remembered for his paintings of the Australian bush and its early pioneers. Some of his best known paintings include *Down on His Luck*, *The Pioneer*, *On the Wallaby Track*, and *A Bush Burial*.

Tom Roberts BORN ▪ 1856   DIED ▪ 1931

Roberts was an artist who was deeply influenced by the bush and its people. His style deviated from more formal compositions of traditional painting. Two of his most famous works include *Shearing the Rams* and *The Big Picture*.

Shearing the Rams (1890)

Arthur Streeton BORN ▪ 1867   DIED ▪ 1943

Painter best known for his light-filled Australian landscapes. Streeton was also an official war artist during the First World War.

Explorer Attacked by Parrots (1960)

Albert Tucker

BORN ▪ 1914   DIED ▪ 1999

Influential modernist painter Albert Tucker's most famous works were painted during the 1940s and dealt with subjects related to the hardships of the Second World War.

Arthur Boyd

Self-portrait (1962–1963)

BORN ▪ 1920   DIED ▪ 1999

Painter Arthur Boyd's work has influenced many international and Australian artists through his depiction of strong landscapes and starkly realised figures. He was named an Officer of the Order of Australia in 1979 and a Companion of the Order of Australia in 1992 in recognition of his contribution to Australian art.

Grace Cossington Smith

BORN ▪ 1892   DIED ▪ 1984

A pioneer of modern painting in Australia, Grace Cossington Smith was the first Australian artist to use post-impressionism in her work, which was characterised by a blend of solid brush strokes and bright natural colours to channel light. She was made an Officer of the Order of the British Empire in 1973 and appointed an Officer of the Order of Australia in 1983 for her services to Australian art.

Self-portrait by Grace Cossington Smith, National Portrait Gallery, Canberra, collection

Emily Kame Kngwarreye

BORN ▪ 1910   DIED ▪ 1996

One of Australia's most significant and successful artists, Kngwarreye (also known as Emily Kam Ngwarray) didn't start painting seriously until she was nearly 80 years old. Her style developed and varied throughout her career, and she is particularly known for her masterpiece *Big Yam Dreaming*, a deeply personal and profound painting that relates to her middle name 'Kame', which refers to the yellow yam flower that grows above the ground.

Albert Namatjira
(1902–1959)

KEY ACHIEVEMENT
Australia's first internationally renowned Indigenous painter

EARLY YEARS

Artist Albert Namatjira was born at Hermannsburg Lutheran Mission near Alice Springs and belonged to the western group of the Arrernte people. Namatjira attended the Hermannsburg mission school, where he was a boarder in a boys' dormitory. At the age of 13 he was initiated into his traditional culture.

Namatjira was interested in art from a young age and sketched the landscape around the mission. In 1934 Namatjira saw an exhibition of landscapes by the artist Rex Battarbee, which was held on the mission, and was inspired to learn landscape painting. In 1936 he accompanied Battarbee on a painting trip to the MacDonnell Ranges.

LANDSCAPES

When Namatjira started painting he quickly developed his own style: a blend of traditional Indigenous colour and technique, and modern landscape painting. He was particularly fond of portrait-style paintings of trees.

Namatjira's first exhibition was held in Melbourne in 1938, followed by sellout shows in Sydney and Adelaide. His work quickly found a following amongst both Indigenous and non-Indigenous people, both in Australia and around the world.

Throughout his career, Namatjira painted around 2000 works.

NOTABLE HONOURS & AWARDS
Queen's Coronation Medal (1953)

The Heide Circle

The Heide Circle was a group of artists who worked at a 15-acre farm called 'Heide', near Heidelberg in Melbourne. Heide was owned by art patrons John and Sunday Reed, who collected Australian art and supported Australian artists by offering them a place to live and work. During the 1930s, 1940s and 1950s, Heide was a home and meeting place for some of Australia's greatest modern painters including Sidney Nolan, Albert Tucker, Joy Hester, John Perceval and Danila Vassilieff.

Sidney Nolan
(1917–1992)

EARLY YEARS

Artist Sidney Nolan was born in Carlton, Victoria. He left school at 14 to study design and crafts at Prahran Technical College in Melbourne. When he was 16, Nolan got a job in the art department of a hat-making company and worked there for six years. In 1934 he began studying at the National Gallery of Victoria Art School.

Nolan had his first solo exhibition in Melbourne in 1940.

NED KELLY SERIES

In the early 1940s Nolan became friends with art patrons John and Sunday Reed, who invited him to stay and work at their home, 'Heide', outside Melbourne. In 1945, during his time at Heide, Nolan began his most famous series of paintings, which were inspired by the bushranger Ned Kelly. Nolan's almost childlike depictions of Kelly have become an iconic part of the bushranger's legend.

In 1951 Nolan moved to London and then travelled around Europe, spending a year in Greece to paint scenes from Greek mythology, as well as time in Paris to study engraving and lithography.

NOTABLE HONOURS & AWARDS

Officer of the Order of the British Empire (1963)

Knight Bachelor (1981)

Member of the Order of Merit (1983)

Companion of the Order of Australia (1988)

❝ Painting is an extension of man's means of communication. As such, it's pure, difficult and wonderful. ❞

– Sidney Nolan

Russell Drysdale
(1912–1981)

EARLY YEARS

Artist Russell Drysdale was born in Sussex, England and immigrated to Melbourne with his family when he was 11 years old.

Although Drysdale went to school in Melbourne, he also spent time in the bush – at his family property in the Riverina district in southern New South Wales and working on his uncle's farm in Queensland.

In his last year at school, Drysdale began drawing and art lessons. The lessons were a form of therapy for one of his eyes, which had a detached retina. In 1930 Drysdale began taking drawing classes from the renowned artist and teacher George Bell. Drysdale studied again with Bell in 1935.

The Drover's Wife (1945)

LANDSCAPES

In 1938 Drysdale had his first solo exhibition before going to London and Paris to work and study. In 1940 he moved back to Australia and settled in Sydney, where he did many of the paintings he is now most famous for, such as *The Drover's Wife* and *Man in a Landscape*. Drysdale developed a reputation for depicting real people in their natural environments, and capturing the spirit of Australian life at that time.

During the 1940s, Drysdale painted a series of works about the drought ravaging the country. He then turned his attention to the gold-mining ghost town of Hill End and the neighbouring town of Sofala. His work depicting Sofala won the Wynne Prize for landscape in 1947. The following year he painted *The Cricketers*, one of the most famous Australian paintings of the twentieth century, which shows three boys playing cricket in a deserted town.

NOTABLE HONOURS & AWARDS

Wynne Prize (1947)

Knighthood (1969)

Companion of the Order of Australia (1980)

Margaret Olley
(1923–2011)

EARLY YEARS

Artist and muse Margaret Olley was born in Lismore, New South Wales. In 1941 she studied art at Brisbane Central Technical College, before moving to Sydney to attend East Sydney Technical College. Olley graduated from East Sydney in 1945 with A-class honours.

Olley was a key member of the vibrant post-war art scene in Sydney. In 1947 she won the first-ever Mosman Art Prize for her painting *New England Landscape*. The following year she had her first solo exhibitions at Macquarie Galleries in Sydney and the Morton Galleries in Queensland.

NOTABLE HONOURS & AWARDS

Mosman Art Prize (1947)

Redcliffe Art Prize (1962; 1963; 1965)

Helena Rubinstein Portrait Prize (1962)

Member of the Order of Australia (1991)

Life Governor of the Art Gallery of NSW (1992)

Companion of the Order of Australia (1996)

STILL-LIFE PAINTING

While many of Olley's contemporaries adopted various art styles throughout their careers, Olley ignored trends and remained primarily committed to still-life painting. She made frequent trips around Australia and overseas, but was always most interested in painting arrangements of flowers, fruit, artefacts and household objects.

Olley was a prolific painter and had more than 90 solo exhibitions during her lifetime.

Throughout her career, Olley donated over 130 paintings to the Art Gallery of New South Wales. Her paintings are also held in the collections of major galleries in Australia and around the world.

Olley was the subject of two Archibald Prize-winning paintings – the first by William Dobell in 1948 and the second by Ben Quilty in 2011. She was also painted by many of her artist friends, including Russell Drysdale.

Still life with pink fish, 1948, Art Gallery of New South Wales © AGNSW

Jeffrey Smart

BORN ▪ 1921 DIED ▪ 2013

Artist Jeffrey Smart is best known for his paintings of bold urban landscapes. Smart trained at the South Australian School of Art between 1937 and 1941 and at the *Académie Montmartre* with painter Fernand Leger in Paris in 1949. His most famous painting, *The Cahill Expressway*, was completed in 1962.

❝ It's not fashionable these days to celebrate life. But I suppose that's what I do. There's no terrible message in it! I have an absolute obsession to paint. I go to bed and can't wait to wake up and be painting again.❞

– Margaret Olley

Brett Whiteley
(1939–1992)

EARLY YEARS

Artist Brett Whiteley was born in Sydney and went to school in Bathurst, New South Wales. He left school at 17 and got a job in a Sydney advertising agency. At the same time, he took night classes in drawing at the Julian Ashton Art School and attended various sketch clubs around the city.

In 1960 Whiteley won an Italian Government travelling scholarship and moved to Italy. He visited London to show his work and was selected to be part of a group show at the prestigious McRoberts and Tunnard Gallery. Whiteley moved to London in November 1960. Soon after that, his work was exhibited at Whitechapel Gallery and one of his paintings was bought by the esteemed Tate Gallery. In 1962 Whiteley had his first solo exhibition, Paintings and Goaches, at the Mathieson Gallery in London.

BODY OF WORK

During his time in London, Whiteley painted a number of his most famous works including *Bathing*, *The Zoo* and *Christies*.

In 1967 Whiteley won a scholarship to study and work in New York. He stayed in the famous Hotel Chelsea and was surrounded by other artists, writers and musicians, painting his impressions of the city. Whiteley also joined the peace movement, actively rallying against involvement in the Vietnam War.

In 1969 Whiteley travelled to Fiji and painted the native people of the island as well as the birdlife. This was the beginning of his love of painting birds, which stayed with him throughout his life. In late 1969 Whiteley returned to Australia and lived at Lavender Bay on Sydney Harbour. Many of his paintings from this time feature the harbour, which he could see from his studio. During this period he also worked on *Alchemy*, one of his best known paintings. It was produced on

NOTABLE
HONOURS & AWARDS

Sir William Angliss
Memorial Art Prize (1975)

Archibald Prize
(1976; 1978)

Sir John Sulman Prize
(1976; 1978)

Wynne Prize
(1977; 1978; 1984)

Member of the Order of
Australia (1991)

18 wood panels and was named for the ancient art of turning ordinary compounds into gold.

PRIZES

Whiteley won the 1976 Archibald Prize for his painting *Self Portrait in Studio*. The following year he won the Wynne Prize for *The Jacaranda Tree (On Sydney Harbour)*. He won the Archibald Prize again in 1978 for *Art, Life and the Other Thing*, as well as the Sulman Prize for *Yellow Nude* and the Wynne Prize for *Summer at Carcoar*.

Pro Hart

BORN ▪ 1928   DIED ▪ 2006

Artist Pro Hart is best known for his unusual painting style, which involved the 'cannon' technique – firing balls of paint at the canvas. Hart was born in Broken Hill, New South Wales and taught himself to paint. He was made a Member of the Order of the British Empire in 1976, and received an Australian Citizen of the Year award in 1983 in recognition of his charity work.

Ken Done

BORN ▪ 1940

Artist Ken done is best known for his simple, brightly coloured images of Australian landmarks. Many of his works are also featured on his popular range of clothing and homewares. Done became a Member of the Order of Australia in 1992 for his services to art, design and tourism.

Frank Hurley

BORN ▪ 1885   DIED ▪ 1962

Photographer and adventurer Frank Hurley is best known for his pioneering images of Douglas Mawson's Antarctic expedition in the early 1900s. He was appointed Officer of the Order of the British Empire and was awarded a Polar Medal in 1941.

Max Dupain

BORN ▪ 1911   DIED ▪ 1992

Renowned photographer Max Dupain's modern style and probing eye documented the world and showed ordinary things in a new light. His visual philosophy developed throughout his career and was exemplified by his major works *Sunbaker* (1937) and *Meat queue* (1946). Dupain was honoured with an Order of the British Empire in 1982.

Only to Taste the Warmth, the Light, the Wind *(1939) by Olive Cotton, courtesy Cotton Family and Josef Lebovic Gallery*

Olive Cotton

BORN ▪ 1911   DIED ▪ 2003

Artistic photographer Olive Cotton worked in the 1930s and 1940s, a time when few women were entering the field. She is best known for her dramatic use of light in images such as *Teacup Ballet* (1935), *Only to Taste the Warmth, the Light, the Wind* (1939), *Max After Surfing* (1938) and *Shasta Daisies* (1937), although her photographs didn't really gain widespread recognition until the 1980s.

Bill Henson

BORN ▪ 1955

Bill Henson is a controversial art photographer whose work has been exhibited in Australia as well as overseas. Henson's photographs are dark, moody and often spark public debate. Henson's work has been collected by every major Australian gallery, and also by leading galleries in America and Europe.

Tracey Moffatt

BORN ▪ 1960

Photographer and video artist Tracy Moffatt's work often focuses on themes of race, history, culture and identity. Her photographs are held in major Australian and international galleries.

Trent Parke

BORN ▪ 1971

Trent Parke is the first and only Australian photographer to have been accepted into the prestigious international photographic co-operative agency Magnum Photo. He has won numerous national and international awards for his work.

> **❝ Dupain's was a modernist sensibility: a belief in progress, the certain knowledge that technology was taking us places and life was improving. It was an extraordinarily pervasive sentiment in the aftermath of total war. ❞**
>
> *– Miriam Cosic on Max Dupain*

Nellie Melba
(1861–1931)

EARLY YEARS

Opera singer Nellie Melba was born as Helen Porter Mitchell in Richmond, Victoria. Melba first studied music at home with her mother and then continued with singing and piano lessons at Presbyterian Ladies' College in Melbourne.

Melba took up singing full-time in 1884. Her first professional performance was in May that year at Melbourne Town Hall, where she received glowing reviews.

In 1886 Melba travelled to London and Paris. In Paris she studied with the famous opera teacher Mathilde Marchesi, who advised her to adopt a stage name. Nellie chose the name 'Melba', a shortened version of 'Melbourne', her home town.

NOTABLE HONOURS & AWARDS
Dame Grand Cross of the Most Excellent Order of the British Empire (1918)

INTERNATIONAL FAME

In 1887, at the age of 26, Melba made her opera debut in a performance of *Rigoletto* in Brussels, Belgium. The performance was a success and she appeared in two more operas in the city. Melba's reputation began to grow and she gained a strong international following.

She sang at Covent Garden in London in 1888, then in Paris the following year, and New York in 1893. Melba continued to appear regularly at Covent Garden throughout the 1890s.

As her reputation grew, Melba was invited to give many private performances to members of high society and royalty around the world. She performed in Russia for Tsar Alexander III, in Stockholm for King Oscar II, in Vienna for Emperor Franz Joseph, in Berlin for Kaiser Wilhelm II and in England for Queen Victoria.

Melba also had a strong following back at home. In 1902 she did a tour of Australia and New Zealand, setting new records for ticket sales of her shows.

Joan Sutherland
(1926–2010)

KEY ACHIEVEMENT
Most acclaimed soprano opera singer of the twentieth century

EARLY YEARS

Opera singer Joan Sutherland was born in Point Piper, New South Wales. After completing school, Sutherland worked as a secretary before being awarded a scholarship to study voice at the age of 18.

In 1949 Sutherland won Australia's most important singing competition, the Sun Aria, and moved to London to study at the Opera School of the Royal College of Music.

LA STUPENDA

In 1952 Sutherland made her debut in *The Magic Flute* at the Royal Opera House in Covent Garden. Two years later she married Australian conductor and pianist Richard Bonynge and he convinced her to explore *bel canto* (Italian for 'beautiful singing') roles that were better suited to her voice than the heavier parts she had been singing. They formed a lasting musical partnership and Bonynge conducted his wife in most of her later appearances.

In 1959 Sutherland was invited to sing *Lucia di Lammermoor* at the Royal Opera House in London. It was a pivotal moment in Sutherland's career and established her as a star.

In 1960 Sutherland recorded the album *The Art of the Prima Donna*, which remains one of the most acclaimed opera albums ever made.

By the early 1960s, Sutherland had sung many famous roles all over the world, including in Venice, where she was nicknamed *La Stupenda*, meaning 'The Stunning One'.

Sutherland's last full-length opera performance was in the role of Marguerite de Valois in *Les Huguenots* at the Sydney Opera House in 1990. She was 63 and the encore she sang was 'Home Sweet Home'.

NOTABLE HONOURS & AWARDS

Commander of the Order of the British Empire (1961)

Australian of the Year (1961)

Companion of the Order of Australia (1975)

Dame Commander of the British Empire (1979)

Order of Merit (1991)

Australian Legends Award (2004)

Robert Helpmann
(1909–1986)

EARLY YEARS

Dancer and choreographer Robert Helpmann was born in Mount Gambier, South Australia. He left school at age 14 and studied ballet with acclaimed dance teacher Nora Stewart. Three years later Helpmann joined a touring Russian ballet company and danced all around Australia.

Helpmann made his professional debut in 1927, when he joined the theatrical company J. C. Williamson and performed as the principal dancer in the comic opera *Frasquita*.

INTERNATIONAL SUCCESS

Helpmann moved to London in 1933 and became principal dancer with the Vic-Wells Ballet. He formed a dancing partnership with ballet star Margot Fonteyn, which was to last for many years. Some consider the highlight of Helpmann's ballet career to be a 1949 tour of the United States, when he and Fonteyn danced the leading roles in *The Sleeping Beauty*.

In the 1940s, Helpmann started acting and producing his own ballets. He also appeared in many films, including *The Red Shoes* in 1948, *The Tales of Hoffmann* in 1951, *Chitty Chitty Bang Bang* in 1968 and *Don Quixote* in 1973.

THE AUSTRALIAN BALLET AND OPERA

In 1965 Helpmann returned to Australia to become co-director of the Australian Ballet. He was made sole director in 1974 and choreographed many ballets including *The Display* and *Sun Music*.

In 1981 Helpmann worked with the Australian Opera, directing Handel's *Alcina*, and in 1983 he celebrated his 60th year in the theatre by producing shows in all three main theatres of the Sydney Opera House.

NOTABLE HONOURS & AWARDS

Commander of the Order of the British Empire (1964)

Australian of the Year (1965)

Knight Bachelor (1968)

Graeme Murphy

BORN - 1950

Dancer and choreographer Graeme Murphy was instrumental in developing the Sydney Dance Company into one of Australia's most successful and well known contemporary dance organisations. Murphy was made a Member of the Order of Australia in 1988 for his service to ballet, and an Officer of the Order of Australia in 2012 for distinguished services to the performing arts.

Bangarra Dance Theatre

Founded in 1989 by Carol Johnson, Bangarra Dance Theatre is Australia's leading indigenous performing arts organisation. Bangarra tells the stories of Indigenous Australians through innovative dance theatre. Bangarra is based in Sydney, but members come from many Aboriginal and Torres Strait Islander clans. Stephen Page has been artistic director of Bangarra since 1991.

"Theatre remains the only thing I understand. It is in the community of the theatre that I have my being. In spite of jealousies and fears, emotional conflicts and human tensions; in spite of the penalty of success and the dread of failure; in spite of tears and feverish gaiety – this is the only life I know. It is the life I love."

– Robert Helpmann

Peter Sculthorpe

BORN - 1929

Composer Peter Sculthorpe is renowned for his orchestral and chamber music that blends Asian, Indigenous Australian and European influences. Sculthorpe was named an Officer of the Order of the British Empire in 1977. He was appointed an Officer of the Order of Australia in 1990, and is a National Living Treasure.

Peter Sculthorpe by Lewis Morley, National Portrait Gallery, Canberra, collection

Richard Tognetti

BORN - 1965

Talented violinist, composer and conductor Richard Tognetti is known for his versatile work. Tognetti is Artistic Director and Leader of the Australian Chamber Orchestra and Artistic Director of the Maribor Festival in Slovenia. He was named a National Living Treasure in 1999, and in 2010 he was appointed an Officer of the Order of Australia for his services to music.

> **❝She could spin lyrical phrases with elegant legato, subtle colourings and expressive nuances.❞**
>
> – New York Times *about Dame Joan Sutherland*

John Bell

BORN ▪ 1940

Actor and theatre director John Bell is the founder of the acclaimed Bell Shakespeare Company. He spent three years with the Royal Shakespeare Company in the United Kingdom and later established the Bell Shakespeare Company in Sydney in 1990. Bell was made an Officer of the Order of the British Empire in 1978, a Member of the Order of Australia in 1987 and an Officer of the Order of Australia in 2009. He has also been named a National Living Treasure.

" It's a secular humanist Bible. There's a lifetime of meditation there, his work is one of the greatest achievements of the human spirit and gives you a hope for humanity itself. "

– John Bell on William Shakespeare

" It's within me to experiment, to dig, to open up the bonnet and fiddle around with the engine – but not to ruin the car, of course. "

– Richard Tognetti

The Helpmann Awards – named after dancer, choreographer and actor **ROBERT HELPMANN** – were established in 2001 to recognise excellence in Australian LIVE performing arts.

Brett Whiteley is the only Australian artist to have won the Archibald, Sulman and Wynne Prizes all in the same year.

Violinist and composer **Richard Tognetti** worked as a violin coach to **Russell Crowe** on the 2003 film *Master and Commander* and won first prize for his film *Musica Surfica* at the 2008 New York Surf Film Festival.

Artistic Director of Bangarra Dance Theatre **STEPHEN PAGE** was NSW Australian of the Year in 2008.

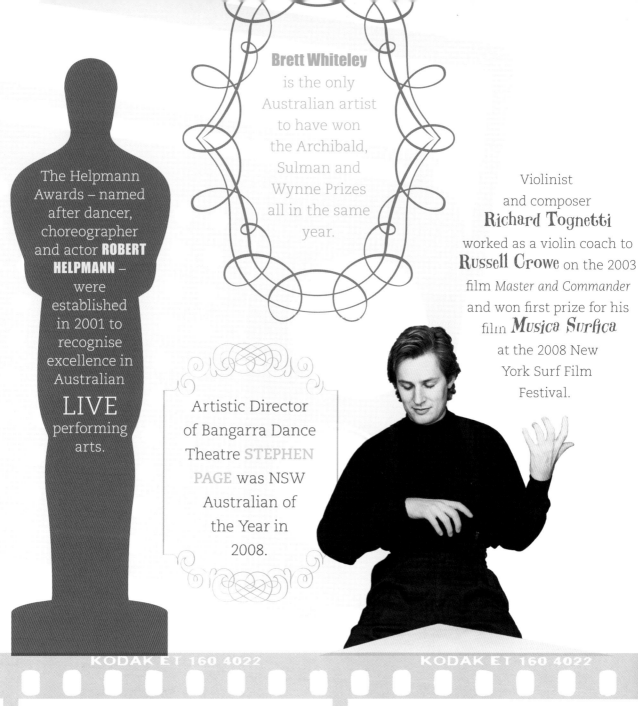

KODAK ET 160 4022   KODAK ET 160 4022

KELVIN COE was the first male ballet dancer to be promoted from chorus member to principal dancer in the Australian Ballet.

LUCETTE ALDOUS was resident principal dancer of the Australian Ballet in the 1970s, and was renowned for her duets with partners such as the legendary Rudolf Nuruyev.

Painter
KEN DONE
is Australia's longest-
serving UNICEF
Goodwill Ambassador.

Antarctic photographer
FRANK HURLEY worked with
the Australian forces during
both world wars, creating
photographic accounts of the
military effort.

In 1920, opera singer
NELLIE MELBA became the
first star to make
live radio broadcasts.

Artist **ALBERT NAMATJIRA**
was the first Indigenous
Australian in the Northern
Territory to be freed from
the legislation that made
Aboriginal people wards
of the state.

KODAK ET 160 4022   KODAK ET 160 4022

Conductor
BERNARD HEINZE
was the first
Australian to
be knighted
for services
to music.

CHARLES MACKERRAS
was the first
Australian chief
conductor of the
Sydney Symphony
Orchestra, and was
the first person to
receive the Queen's
Medal for Music.

24   24

"I love a sunburnt country,
A land of sweeping plains,
Of ragged mountain ranges,
Of droughts and flooding rains."

– Dorothea Mackellar, 'My Country'

Banjo Paterson
(1864–1941)

EARLY YEARS

Poet and journalist Banjo Paterson was born at Narrambla in rural New South Wales. His family later moved to Yass, where Paterson's parents ran Illalong Station. Although he went to school in Sydney from the age of ten, Paterson returned to the station during school breaks and maintained a strong connection to the Australian bush.

When he was 16, Paterson began working in a law firm and eventually became a qualified solicitor. In his early 20s he co-founded the legal firm Street and Paterson, and also began writing verse for *The Bulletin* magazine and the *Sydney Mail*. His first poem, 'El Mahdi to the Australian Troops', was published in *The Bulletin* in 1885.

'THE MAN FROM SNOWY RIVER' AND 'WALTZING MATILDA'

Paterson's reputation as a poet continued to grow over the next ten years, and in 1890 he published his now famous poem 'The Man from Snowy River', about the search for a prizewinning racehorse that has escaped.

His first book, *The Man from Snowy River and Other Verses*, was published in 1895 and was an instant success. The first edition sold out in one week and four further editions were published within six months. His second book of verse, *Old Bush Songs*, was published to great acclaim in 1905.

In 1903 Paterson achieved national and international recognition with the publication of his iconic ballad 'Waltzing Matilda'. He wrote the ballad in 1895 and it was originally performed as a song.

In addition to poetry, Paterson wrote news articles. In 1899 he became a war correspondent for the *Sydney Morning Herald*, documenting the Second Boer War in South Africa, as well as the Chinese Boxer Rebellion.

NOTABLE HONOURS & AWARDS

Commander of the British Empire (1939)

During the First World War, Paterson travelled to Europe as a correspondent, but was recruited as an ambulance driver instead. He was injured in 1916 and thought to be missing in action, but was brought back to Australia in 1919.

Saltbush Bill, J.P. and Other Verses, Banjo's third volume of poetry, was published in 1917. In 1922 he was appointed editor of the racing journal *Sydney Sportsman*.

As well as his poetry and journalism, Banjo also wrote two novels, *An Outback Marriage* in 1906 and *The Shearer's Colt* in 1936, as well as many short stories.

Marcus Clarke

BORN ▪ 1846 DIED ▪ 1881

Novelist and poet Marcus Clarke is best known for his 1874 novel *For the Term of his Natural Life*, about a young man transported to Australia as a convict for a crime he did not commit.

Mary Gilmore

BORN ▪ 1865 DEATH ▪ 1962

Poet and journalist Mary Gilmore is a literary icon, who is also known for her work as an advocate of the rights of women, children and Indigenous Australians. Gilmore published six books of poems and three of prose, as well as a memoir and many newspaper articles. She was appointed a Dame Commander of the Order of the British Empire in 1937, becoming the first person to be granted this award for services to literature.

Henry Lawson
(1867–1922)

EARLY YEARS

Writer and poet Henry Lawson was born in Grenfell, New South Wales. He didn't attend school until he was nine years old because there was no local schoolhouse before that time. In the same year he started school, Lawson began to lose his hearing, and by the time he was 14 he was almost completely deaf. Lawson left school after three years to work with his father on local building jobs.

In 1883 Lawson moved to Sydney and began an apprenticeship with a coach painter. He began taking night classes so he could finish his schooling, and it was around this time that he started writing fiction and poetry.

WRITING CAREER

In 1887 Lawson had his first poem, 'A Song of the Republic', published in *The Bulletin* magazine in Sydney. He had several more poems published over the next few years and his reputation as a writer of verse began to grow.

Lawson was offered work writing articles and verse for *Boomerang* magazine in Brisbane in 1890. But when *Boomerang* folded the following year, Lawson returned to Sydney and continued to write for *The Bulletin*. His acclaimed short story 'The Drover's Wife' was published during this time.

In 1892 *The Bulletin* sent Lawson on assignment to drought-affected regional New South Wales to gather first-hand material for his magazine stories, as well as his own fiction pieces. This experience confirmed Lawson's opinion about the harsh reality of the Australian bush and had a big influence on his writing. His two bestselling collections of verse, *While the Billy Boils* and *In the Days When the World Was Wide and Other Verses*, were published in 1896 and contained reflections about his time on assignment in the bush.

Henry Handel Richardson
(1870–1946)

KEY ACHIEVEMENT
One of Australia's first successful female authors, who wrote *The Getting of Wisdom* and *The Fortunes of Richard Mahony*

EARLY YEARS

Henry Handel Richardson was the pseudonym of writer Ethel Florence Lindesay Richardson. She was born in Fitzroy, Victoria and attended boarding school at the Presbyterian Ladies' College in Melbourne from the age of 13. In 1889 Richardson moved to Germany with her family, where she studied piano at the Royal Conservatorium.

WRITING CAREER

Richardson began writing when she married and moved to London in 1903.

There were very few female authors in the 1900s, so Richardson adopted the masculine pen name of Henry Handel Richardson to improve her chances of being published.

Richardson's first novel, *Maurice Guest*, was published in 1908. The novel was not well reviewed in the United Kingdom, but was praised when it was translated into German.

Her second – and most famous – novel, *The Getting of Wisdom*, was published in 1910 and has been in print ever since. Based on Richardson's own life, the novel tells the story of an unspoiled country girl who feels out of place when she is sent to a posh boarding school in Melbourne after her family falls on hard times.

Richardson briefly returned to Australia in 1912 to research her famous trilogy *The Fortunes of Richard Mahony*. The first volume, *Australia Felix*, was published in 1917, the second instalment, *The Way Home*, in 1925 and the final book, *Ultima Thule*, in 1929. The third volume was a huge success and all three books were published together in 1930.

KEY ACHIEVEMENT
Author of the classic
poem 'My Country'

Dorothea Mackellar
(1885–1968)

EARLY YEARS

Poet Dorothea Mackellar was born in Point Piper, New South Wales. She was mostly educated at home by private tutors. Growing up, Mackellar travelled extensively with her family and was able to speak several languages. She also spent a lot of time in regional New South Wales, staying at her family's properties in Gunnedah and the Hunter Valley.

'MY COUNTRY'

Mackellar began writing poetry from a young age. Her first, and most famous poem, 'Core of My Heart,' was published in 1905. Mackellar wrote the poem, which is now better known under the title 'My Country,' while she was travelling in England and feeling homesick for Australia. The poem was inspired by Mackellar's childhood visits to rural New South Wales, and captures the mood of the country just before the break of a long drought. Although 'My Country' was first published in a London newspaper, it was soon reprinted many times in Australian newspapers and became a symbol of Australian national identity.

In 1911, 'My Country' was included in Mackellar's first volume of verse, *The Closed Door*. She also published *The Witch Maid, and Other Verses* in 1914, *Dreamharbour* in 1923 and *Fancy Dress* in 1926.

May Gibbs
(1877–1969)

KEY ACHIEVEMENT
Wrote and illustrated the children's classic *The Complete Adventures of Snugglepot and Cuddlepie*

EARLY YEARS

Children's author Cecilia 'May' Gibbs was born in Kent in the United Kingdom and moved to Western Australia with her family when she was four years old. Gibbs went to school in Perth, but in 1901 she returned to England to study art.

Gibbs came back to Australia in 1913 and settled in Sydney. She earned a living as a freelance illustrator, while also developing her own writing and illustration projects.

THE COMPLETE ADVENTURES OF SNUGGLEPOT AND CUDDLEPIE

In 1916 Gibbs published the first book about her now famous gumnut characters. It was called *The Gumnut Babies* and featured Australian bush fairies. It was quickly followed by other little books with similar flower fairies. Gibbs also produced a range of bush baby bookmarks and stationery.

In 1918, *Tales of Snugglepot and Cuddlepie: Their Adventures Wonderful* was published and became a bestseller. Snugglepot and Cuddlepie, two cute gumnut babies, appeared in other successful books, including a collection called *The Complete Adventures of Snugglepot and Cuddlepie*. The books have become Australian classics and are still in print today.

Gibbs left the copyright and all future earnings from the designs of her gumnut characters and her stories to Northcott Disability Services and Cerebral Palsy Alliance, with the money going towards helping children in need. Gibbs's house, Nutcote Cottage, has been turned into a museum, as well as a retreat for children's writers.

Norman Lindsay
(1879–1969)

EARLY YEARS

Writer and artist Norman Lindsay was born in Creswick, Victoria. He went to Creswick Grammar School and developed an interest in art from a very early age after visiting the art gallery in Ballarat with his grandfather.

When he was 16, Lindsay moved to Melbourne to work as a newspaper and magazine illustrator. In 1901 he relocated to Sydney and started working for *The Bulletin*, where he continued to work as a writer and illustrator for the next 50 years.

THE MAGIC PUDDING

Although Lindsay is known as one of Australia's greatest artists, he is also famous for writing children's books. *The Magic Pudding: Being the Adventures of Bunyip Bluegum and his friends Bill Barnacle and Sam Sawnoff* is perhaps his most famous work and was published in 1918. The book, which was also illustrated by Lindsay, is about the adventures of three friends who own a magic pudding that never runs out. The friends have to defend the pudding from thieves who want it for themselves.

ART

Lindsay was one of Australia's most prolific artists, producing pen-and-ink drawings, etchings, watercolours, oil paintings, and bronze and concrete sculptures. He delighted in depicting the nude human body in all forms of his work. A huge collection of his possessions, books and artwork is displayed in his former Faulconbridge home in the Blue Mountains, now the Norman Lindsay Gallery and Museum.

Miles Franklin
(1879–1954)

EARLY YEARS

Novelist Miles Franklin was born in Talbingo, New South Wales. She lived on a property called Brindabella Station until she was ten years old, and was taught at home during this time. All of her tutors and teachers recognised Franklin's talent and encouraged her to write.

MY BRILLIANT CAREER AND OTHER WORK

Franklin wrote her first and best known novel, *My Brilliant Career*, when she was only 20 years old. It was published two years later with the help of poet Henry Lawson. The book tells the story of a rebellious and spirited teenage girl called Sybylla Melvyn, who shared many similarities with Miles Franklin herself, growing up in the Australian outback in the 1890s. The book was an instant success and established Franklin as one of the greatest Australian writers of her time.

In 1906 Franklin left Australia for the United States, where she worked as a secretary and wrote a number of novels before travelling to England in 1915. She worked as a hospital cook in Europe during the Second World War and continued to write.

Franklin returned to Australia in 1932 and wrote a number of historical bush novels using the name 'Brent of Bin Bin'. She also wrote *All That Swagger* under her real name.

THE MILES FRANKLIN LITERARY AWARD

Franklin was a member of a number of writing groups and always supported and mentored other writers. When she died she left enough money to establish an annual literary award, known as The Miles Franklin Award, which continues today. The first winner was Patrick White with his 1957 novel, *Voss*.

Patrick White
(1912-1990)

EARLY YEARS

Novelist Patrick White was born in Knightsbridge, England and moved to Sydney with his family when he was six months old. Suffering chronic asthma as a child, White was sent to boarding school in the Southern Highlands of New South Wales in the hope that his health would improve. In 1924 White went to boarding school in England, where he started to write poems and plays. Returning to Australia in 1928, White spent two years working as a stockman on a station near the Snowy Mountains. From 1932 to 1935 he lived in England again, studying French and German literature at Cambridge University.

WRITING CAREER

While at Cambridge, White published a collection of poetry called *The Ploughman and Other Poems* (1934), and wrote a play titled *Bread and Butter Women* (1935). His first novel, *Happy Valley*, was published in 1939.

White served in the British Royal Air Force during the Second World War, returning to Australia in late 1947.

In 1955, White's novels *The Aunt's Story* and *The Tree of Man* were published. Although *The Tree of Man* was a hit in America, it was not warmly received in Australia. But his next novel, *Voss* (1957), won the first-ever Miles Franklin Literary Award for excellence in Australian literature, and in 1961 *Riders in the Chariot* also won the award. In 1970 White published his extraordinary novel *The Vivisector*, which tells the story of an artist. The book won the 1973 Nobel Prize for Literature and is the only Australian to have won this award.

White was made Australian of the Year in 1974 and the sales of his book increased. In 1979 *The Twyborn Affair* was shortlisted for the prestigious Man Booker Prize, but later

NOTABLE HONOURS & AWARDS

Nobel Prize (1973)

Australian of the Year (1974)

removed from the list at White's own request – he believed the award should go to a younger and more deserving author, and had a general dislike of literary awards.

White published his autobiography, *Flaws in the Glass: a self-portrait*, in 1981 and released his novel *Memoirs of Many in One* in 1986. In 2012 *The Hanging Garden*, an unfinished novel, was published 22 years after White's death.

Kenneth Slessor

BORN ▪ 1901   DIED ▪ 1971

Kenneth Slessor was a poet and journalist best known for introducing a modernist style to Australian poetry. Slessor's most renowned poems are 'Five Bells', about the death of one of his friends, and 'Beach Burial', about the Australian troops who fought in the Second World War.

> **"Uncle first said that he was glad to see I had the spirit of an Australian, and then threatened to put my nose above my chin if I failed to behave properly. Grannie remarked that I might have the spirit of an Australian, but I had by no means the manners of a lady..."**
>
> – Miles Franklin, *My Brilliant Career*

Christina Stead
(1902–1983)

EARLY YEARS

Writer Christina Stead was born in Rockdale, New South Wales. After school she won a scholarship to teachers' college and graduated in 1921. The following year Stead worked as a research assistant and studied psychology at the University of Sydney. She taught for two years, but did not enjoy it and resigned in 1925. For the next few years Stead worked as a secretary and also began writing. In 1928 she moved to England and then to Paris in 1929.

WRITING CAREER

Stead's first two books, *Seven Poor Men of Sydney* and *The Salzburg Tales*, were published in London in 1934. They were well received and Stead's third book, *All Nations*, came out in 1938.

Stead moved to America in 1937 and three years later her best known novel, *The Man Who Loved Children,* was published. The book, about a dysfunctional family and a domineering father, is loosely based on Stead's own childhood, although it is set in the United States. *The Man Who Loved Children* received negative reviews and sold very few copies when it was first published. But in 1965 the book was re-released and gained widespread popularity and critical acclaim. In 2005 *Time* magazine included it on their list of '100 Best Novels from 1923 to 2005'.

Stead published 14 novels in her lifetime. Her last book, *I'm Dying Laughing*, had not been published when she died in 1983, but was later released in 1986.

**NOTABLE
HONOURS & AWARDS**

Patrick White Literary
Award (1974)

**❝I don't know what imagination is,
if not an unpruned, tangled kind of memory.❞**

– Christina Stead, Letty Fox: Her Luck

Manning Clark
(1915–1991)

KEY ACHIEVEMENT
Author of *A History of Australia*

EARLY YEARS

Historian and writer Manning Clark was born in Burwood, New South Wales. In 1928 he won a scholarship to Melbourne Grammar School. Clark graduated from Melbourne University, with first-class honours in History and Political Science in 1938. In that same year, Clark travelled to England to continue his studies at Oxford University. He returned to Australia in 1944 and completed his Master of Arts degree at Melbourne University.

In 1949 Clark accepted a position as Professor of History at Canberra University College. In 1972 he was appointed to the new post of Professor of Australian History, which he held until he retired in 1974. Clark retained the title Emeritus Professor until he died.

A HISTORY OF AUSTRALIA AND OTHER WORK

In 1955 Clark began researching his impressive six-volume work, *A History of Australia*. The first volume, *History: From the Earliest Times to the Age of Macquarie*, was published in 1962. The sixth and final volume was published 25 years later in 1987.

A History of Australia remains the most ambitious and comprehensive body of work about Australian history. The project has been praised for its breadth and scope, but also criticised for being subjective and containing too many of Clark's personal views about history.

In addition to the huge achievement of writing and researching *A History of Australia* over many years, Clark also worked on other writing projects. His last works were two volumes of his autobiography, *The Puzzles of Childhood,* published in 1989 and *The Quest for Grace,* published in 1990. He was in the middle of writing the third volume, *A Historian's Apprenticeship,* when he died.

NOTABLE HONOURS & AWARDS

Companion of the Order of Australia (1975)

Henry Lawson Arts Award (1969)

Australian Literature Society's Gold Medal (1970)

Age Book Prize (1974)

New South Wales Premier's Literary Award (1979)

Australian of the Year (1980)

Judith Wright

BORN ▪ 1915 DIED ▪ 2000

Accomplished poet Judith Wright was passionate about protecting the environment and campaigning for Aboriginal land rights, and these themes recurred throughout her work. Wright's first book of poetry, *The Moving Image*, was published in 1946. She was the second Australian to receive the Queen's Gold Medal for Poetry, which she was awarded in 1992, and in 1994 Wright won the Human Rights and Equal Opportunity Commission Poetry Award for her *Collected Poems*.

Ray Lawler

BORN ▪ 1921

Playwright Ray Lawler is best known for his play *The Summer of the Seventeenth Doll*, which he wrote in 1953 and which had its stage premiere in 1955. The play is notable for being one of the first to portray naturalistic Australian settings and characters.

David Malouf

BORN ▪ 1934

Accomplished writer David Malouf has won a number of international prizes for his work, including the first-ever Australia-Asia Literary Award in 2008 for his book *Collected Stories*. Malouf's other popular works include the award-winning *The Great World* (1990), *Remembering Babylon* (1993), which was shortlisted for the Man Booker Prize, and his short-story collection *Every Move You Make* (2007). In 2008, Malouf won the Australian Publishers Association's prestigious Lloyd O'Neil Award for outstanding service to the Australian book industry and was elected a Fellow of the Royal Society of Literature in the same year.

Tom Keneally

BORN ▪ 1935

An internationally acclaimed writer of novels, plays and non-fiction, Tom Keneally won the Man Booker Prize in 1982 for his best known book *Schindler's Ark*, which was later made into an Academy Award-winning film. Keneally has been shortlisted for the Man Booker Prize four times and won the Miles Franklin Award twice for his books *Bring Larks and Heroes* and *Three Cheers for the Paraclete*. Keneally was appointed an Officer of the Order of Australia in 1983 for his services to Australian literature, and was elected a National Living Treasure in 1997.

Robert Hughes

BORN ▪ 1938   DIED ▪ 2012

Robert Hughes was an internationally renowned art critic, and writer and producer of television documentaries. Hughes was made an Officer of the Order of Australia in 1991 and was named as National Living Treasure.

Les Murray

BORN ▪ 1938

Regarded as one of the finest living poets writing in English, Les Murray is also a critic and editor of poetry anthologies. He has published an expansive range of work over his 40-year career – 30 volumes of poetry, two verse novels and collections of his prose writings – and has received many awards, such as the 1984 Kenneth Slessor Prize for Poetry for *The People's Other World*. In 1989 he was appointed an Officer of the Order of Australia for services to Australian literature and was named a National Living Treasure in 1997.

Germaine Greer

BORN ▪ 1939

Feminist and writer Germaine Greer's opinion pieces and lectures have a worldwide audience. Her book *The Female Eunuch* caused controversy at the time of its release in 1970, but went on to become an international bestseller.

Colleen McCullough

BORN ▪ 1937

Australian writer best known for her 1977 novel *The Thorn Birds*, a sweeping family saga set in the Australian outback. In 2006 McCullough was awarded an Order of Australia for her services to the arts as an author, and to the community through roles supporting national and international educational programs.

Helen Garner

BORN ▪ 1942

Journalist and author of both fiction and non-fiction books, Garner is well known for writing about her own experiences. She has won a number of awards, including a National Book Council Award in 1978 for her first novel, *Monkey Grip*, a Walkley Award for her journalism, various state Premier's Literary Awards, and the 2006 Melbourne Prize for Literature.

David Williamson

BORN ▪ 1942

One of Australia's best known playwrights, David Williamson has written more than 40 plays. A few of Williamson's most famous works include *The Removalists* (1971), *Don's Party* (1971) and *Dead White Males* (1995). He has received four Australian Film Institute Awards, as well as many other film and theatre honours.

Peter Carey

BORN ▪ 1943

Peter Carey is an award-winning author. He is one of only four writers to have won the Man Booker Prize twice, in 1988 for *Oscar and Lucinda*, and in 2001 for *True History of the Kelly Gang*. His other famous novels include *Bliss* (1981) and *Illywhacker* (1985). Carey has also won the Miles Franklin Award three times and was named an Officer of the Order of Australia in 2012.

Peter Singer

BORN ▪ 1946

Writer Peter Singer's work about moral issues has incited both admiration and controversy. He is most famous for his book *Animal Liberation*, published in 1975. He was named a Companion of the Order of Australia in 2012 for his contribution to philosophy and literature.

"You could not tell a story like this. A story like this you could only feel."

– *Peter Carey, Oscar and Luinda*

Oodgeroo Noonuccal
(1920–1993)

EARLY YEARS

Poet, artist, teacher and activist Oodgeroo Noonuccal was born on North Stradbroke Island in South-East Queensland. She was known as Kath Walker until 1988, when she adopted the traditional name of Oodgeroo ('paperbark tree') and her tribal name of Noonuccal.

Noonuccal went to a local school until she left at age 13 to become a domestic servant in Brisbane. During the Second World War, Noonuccal enlisted in the Australian Women's Army Service (AWAS) and worked in switchboard operations. She was forced to leave the AWAS in 1943 when a serious ear infection left her partially deaf.

WRITING CAREER

In the 1950s, Noonuccal started writing poetry and joined a Brisbane writers' group. In 1963, she sent a collection of poems to a Brisbane publisher and her book *We Are Going* was published the next year. It was an instant bestseller. Readers related to her honest style with its no-nonsense element of protest for a better life for Indigenous people. Her second collection, *The Dawn is at Hand*, was published in 1966 and a third collection, *My People: A Kath Walker Collection*, appeared in 1970.

Noonuccal also published a number of books of Aboriginal legends for young readers, including *Stradbroke Dreamtime* in 1972, *Father Sky and Mother Earth* in 1981 and *The Rainbow Serpent* in 1988. These were designed to give an insight into Aboriginal culture and to promote the storytelling tradition in a way all Australians could understand.

TEACHING

Noonuccal established the Noonuccal-Nughie Education and Cultural Centre on Stradbroke Island, where it quickly became a hub for visiting Aboriginal students from around the country. During this time she also travelled widely, lecturing in Australia and overseas.

INDIGENOUS RIGHTS

Throughout the 1960s, Noonuccal was at the forefront of the campaign to get voting rights and Australian citizenship for Indigenous Australians, which were achieved in 1965 and 1967 respectively.

NOTABLE HONOURS & AWARDS

Mary Gilmore Medal (1970)

Fellowship of Australian Writers' Award

Member of the Order of the British Empire (1970) – subsequently returned

Sally Morgan

BORN ▪ 1951

Sally Morgan is one of Australia's best known Indigenous writers and artists. Morgan didn't know she was Aboriginal until she was 15, and her 1987 autobiography *My Place* chronicles her search to find out more about her family and their past. *My Place* was awarded the 1987 Human Rights Award for Literature and Other Writing. Morgan has written for both adults and children and has won numerous awards for her work.

Tim Winton

BORN ▪ 1960

Internationally acclaimed writer Tim Winton's work is firmly set in the Australian landscape. Some of his popular works include *Cloudstreet* (1991), the children's series *Lockie Leonard*, and *Breath* (2008). Winton has won the Miles Franklin Award four times, and his novels *The Riders* (1995) and *Dirt Music* (2002) were shortlisted for the Man Booker Prize. He has been named a National Living Treasure and was awarded the Centenary Medal for his service to literature and the community.

In 2003 writer
TIM WINTON
was awarded the first-ever
Australian Society of Authors
Medal in recognition of his work
on the campaign to save the
Ningaloo Reef.

Before becoming
a writer, **PETER CAREY** worked in
advertising and helped produce
campaigns for clients such as
the automobile company
Volkswagen,
Lindeman's Wine
and many others.

Poet Judith Wright
felt strongly about
Aboriginal land rights
and wrote letters to
Prime Minister John
Howard, among others,
asking for reform.

During
award-winning
writer **PATRICK
WHITE'S** time
serving in the British
Royal Air Force, he
was sent to the
Middle East as
an intelligence
officer.

MILES FRANKLIN'S *My Brilliant Career* was initially rejected for publication in Australia. It was first published in Britain, by **William Blackwood & Sons**, in 1901.

In 1974 writer and political activist **OODGEROO NOONUCCAL** was on board a flight hijacked by Palestinian liberation militants. During her captivity she wrote two poems, 'Commonplace' and 'Yusuf (Hijacker)', in pencil on a sick bag.

Philosophical writer **PETER SINGER** was inducted into the United States **ANIMAL RIGHTS HALL OF FAME** in 2000.

CHRISTINA STEAD has two awards named in her honour: The New South Wales Premier's Christina Stead Prize for Fiction and the Fellowship of Australian Writers.

"Never be afraid to laugh at yourself. After all, you could be missing out on the joke of the century."

– *Dame Edna Everage*

ENTERTAINMENT

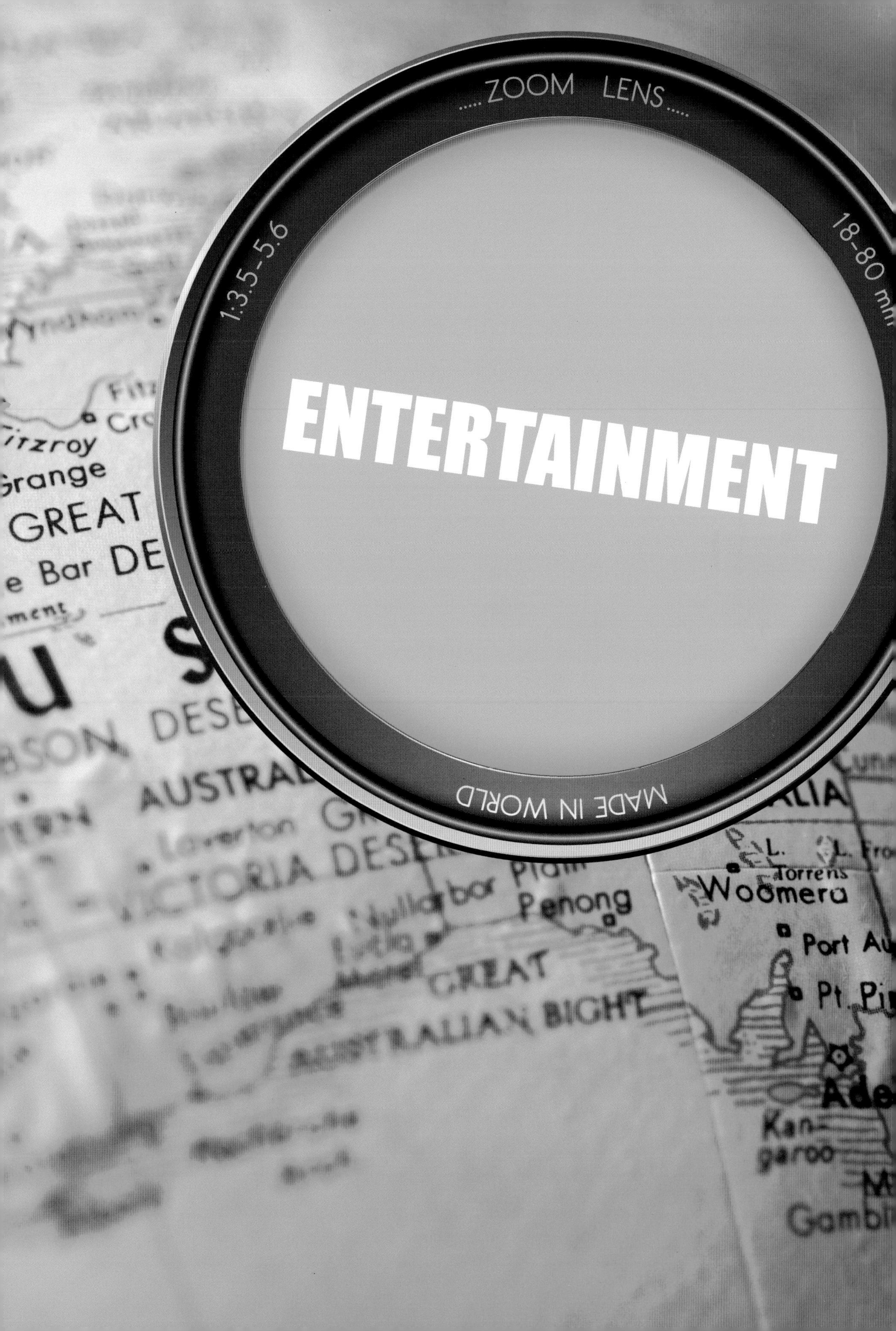

Louise Nellie Lovely

BORN ▪ 1895   DIED ▪ 1980

Louise Nellie Lovely was the first Australian movie actress to find success in America. Lovely started acting when she was nine and went on to have a successful career as a child actress. She moved to America at the age of 19 and was signed up by Universal Studios. Lovely soon became one of their star actresses.

Judith Anderson

BORN ▪ 1898   DEATH ▪ 1992

An international stage and screen performer, Judith Anderson had her first big success on Broadway in New York with the play *The Cobra* in 1924. She also starred in films such as *Rebecca* (1940) and *Cat on a Hot Tin Roof* (1958), and the television show *Santa Barbara* (1984). Anderson was made a Dame of the British Empire in 1960 for her contribution to the performing arts.

Errol Flynn

BORN ▪ 1909   DIED ▪ 1959

Hollywood star from the 1930s to the 1950s, Australian actor Errol Flynn was well known for his roles as the romantic lead. Some of his more famous movies include *Captain Blood* (1935), *The Charge of the Light Brigade* (1936) and *The Adventures of Robin Hood* (1938).

Ruth Cracknell

BORN ▪ 1925 DIED ▪ 2002

Award-winning Australian film, television and theatre actress Ruth Cracknell is best known for her role in the long-running television series *Mother and Son*. She was made a Member of the Order of Australia in 1990.

Paul Hogan

BORN ▪ 1939

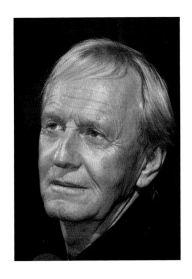

An actor and comedian known for his larrikin sense of humour, Paul Hogan became internationally recognised through a series of ads he did for Australian beer and tourism. He also starred in his own sketch program *The Paul Hogan Show,* and is perhaps most famous for his role as Mick in the *Crocodile Dundee* film series. Hogan was made Australian of the Year and appointed Member of the Order of Australia in 1985.

Judy Davis

BORN ▪ 1955

Award-winning actress Judy Davis is best known in Australian cinema for her role as Sybylla Melvyn, the main character in the film adaptation of *My Brilliant Career* (1979). In total, Davis has won two Golden Globe awards, three Emmy awards, two BAFTA awards and seven Australian Film Institute (AFI) Awards. She has also been nominated for two Academy Awards.

Russell Crowe

BORN • 1964

New Zealand-born actor Russell Crowe won the 2000 Academy Award for Best Actor for his role in *Gladiator*. He was also nominated for *The Insider* (1999) and *A Beautiful Mind* (2001). Crowe has a star on the Hollywood Walk of Fame in honour of his contribution to commercial film.

Hugh Jackman

BORN • 1968

Award-winning actor Hugh Jackman is known for his work in film, television and musical theatre. Jackman received a Tony Award for the role of Peter Allen in the stage musical *The Boy from Oz*, and won the 2012 Golden Globe Award for Best Actor (Comedy or Musical) for his performance in the film adaption of the musical *Les Misérables*.

Nicole Kidman

BIRTH • 1967

Actress Nicole Kidman was the first Australian to win an Academy Award for Best Actress for her performance in *The Hours* (2002). Some of her other popular film roles include *Days of Thunder, Cold Mountain*, as well as *Moulin Rouge* and *Australia*. Kidman has a star on the Hollywood Walk of Fame and was made a Companion of the Order of Australia in 2006.

Cate Blanchett
(1969–)

KEY ACHIEVEMENT
Won the 2004 Academy Award for Best Actress

EARLY YEARS

Film and theatre actress Cate Blanchett was born in Victoria and studied at the University of Melbourne before enrolling in the National Institute of Dramatic Art (NIDA).

ACTING CAREER

Blanchett's first big theatre role was in the 1992 production of *Oleanna*, in which she starred opposite Geoffrey Rush. Soon she began taking on cinematic roles such Elizabeth I of England in *Elizabeth* (1998) and Katharine Hepburn in *The Aviator* (2004), for which she won an Academy Award.

Blanchett has a star on the Hollywood Walk of Fame and in 2007 *Time* magazine named her as one of the '100 Most Influential People in the World'. As well as her achievements in film, Blanchett is also heavily associated with the theatre. From 2008 to 2013, she was joint Artistic Director of the Sydney Theatre Company with her husband, Andrew Upton.

NOTABLE HONOURS & AWARDS

Sydney Theatre Critics Circle Best Newcomer of the Year (1993)

Academy Award for Best Supporting Actress (2004)

> **❝If you know you are going to fail, then fail gloriously.❞**
>
> *– Cate Blanchett*

Bruce Beresford
BORN▪1940

Academy Award-nominated director Bruce Beresford's major Hollywood films include *Tender Mercies* (1984), *Driving Miss Daisy* (1990) and *Mao's Last Dancer* (2009). Beresford's films *Don's Party* (1976) and *Breaker Morant* (1980) are considered Australian classics.

Jim Sharman

BORN ▪ 1945

Theatre director Jim Sharman is best known for his productions of musicals such as *Hair*, *Jesus Christ Superstar* and *The Rocky Horror Picture Show*, which were considered radical and risqué for the late 1960s and early 1970s when they were first performed.

Geoffrey Rush

BORN ▪ 1951

Geoffrey Rush is the first Australian-born actor to win an Academy Award for Best Actor, which he received for his role in *Shine* (1996). He has also received a Tony Award, an Emmy Award, three British Academy Awards (BAFTAs) and four Screen Guild Awards. His best known films include *Shine* (1996), *Elizabeth* (1998), *Pirates of the Caribbean: The Curse of the Black Pearl* (2003) and *The King's Speech* (2010). Rush was appointed foundation President of the Academy of Cinema and Television Arts in 2011, and was named Australian of the Year in 2012.

> **❝I do love perusing the dictionary to find how many words I don't use – words that have specific, sharp, focused meaning. I also love the sound of certain words. I love the sound of the word pom-pom.❞**
>
> *– Geoffrey Rush*

Peter Weir

BORN ▪ 1944

Movie director Peter Weir has achieved worldwide recognition for a range of films such as *Picnic at Hanging Rock* (1975), *Gallipoli* (1981), *Witness* (1985), *Dead Poets Society* (1989), *The Truman Show* (1998) and *Master and Commander: The Far Side of the World* (2003). Weir has received a number of Academy Award nominations throughout his career and was appointed a Member of the Order of Australia in 1982 for his service to the film industry.

George Miller

BORN ▪ 1945

Director George Miller was made popular by his cult film series *Mad Max*, featuring Mel Gibson. Miller's other well known movies include *Babe: Pig in the City* (1998), *Lorenzo's Oil* (1992), *The Witches of Eastwick* (1987) and the musical animation *Happy Feet* (2006), which won the Academy Award for Best Animated Feature in 2007. Miller was appointed Officer of the Order of Australia in 1996.

Phillip Noyce

BORN ▪ 1950

Director Phillip Noyce's major Hollywood films include *Dead Calm* (1989), *Clear and Present Danger* (1994) and *The Bone Collector* (1999). Noyce's 1978 feature film *Newsfront* won the Australian Film Institute (AFI) Award for Best Film, Director, and Screenplay. In 2002 his movie *Rabbit-Proof Fence* won the AFI Award for Best Film.

Gillian Armstrong

BORN ▪ 1950

Film director Gillian Armstrong's adaptation of Miles Franklin's literary classic *My Brilliant Career* (1979) received an Academy Award nomination for Best Achievement in Costume Design. Some of Armstrong's other memorable films include *Little Women* (1994), *Oscar and Lucinda* (1997) and *Unfolding Florence* (2006), a documentary on Australian designer Florence Broadhurst.

Jan Chapman

BORN ▪ 1950

Film producer Jan Chapman has worked on a number of iconic Australian films such as *The Last Days of Chez Nous* (1992), *The Piano* (1993) and *Lantana* (2001). Chapman has been nominated for an AFI Award as well as an Academy Award.

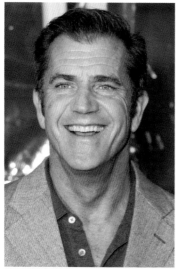

Mel Gibson

BORN ▪ 1956

Actor and director Mel Gibson has starred in blockbuster film franchises such as *Mad Max* and *Lethal Weapon*. Gibson studied acting at the NIDA in Sydney and played leading stage and television roles before moving to film. He has produced, directed and starred in a number of movies, including the 1995 film *Braveheart*, for which he won the Academy Award for Best Director. In 1997 he was named an Officer of the Order of Australia for his service to the Australian film industry.

Neil Armfield

BORN▪1955

Director Neil Armfield played a crucial role in the formation of Sydney's Belvoir St Theatre. In 1989 he won an AFI Award for Best Direction in a Mini-Series for *Eden's Lost*. Some of Armfield's theatrical highlights are the world tour of *Cloudstreet* (adapted from Tim Winton's novel), and the opera *Bliss* (based on Peter Carey's novel) for Opera Australia. In 2005 he directed and co-wrote the feature film *Candy* (adapted from the novel by Luke Davies), which won two awards for best adapted screenplay. In 2007 Armfield was made on Officer of the Order of Australia.

Baz Luhrmann

BORN▪1962

Director Baz Luhrmann is known worldwide for his visually vibrant films. Luhrmann graduated from NIDA in 1985 and is best known for his movies *Strictly Ballroom* (1992), *Romeo and Juliet* (1996), *Moulin Rouge!* (2001), *Australia* (2008) and *The Great Gatsby* (2013).

> **❝If Paris is a city of lights, Sydney is the city of fireworks.❞**
>
> *– Baz Luhrmann*

Barry Humphries
(1934–)

EARLY YEARS

Entertainer Barry Humphries was born in Kew, Victoria. He studied law at Melbourne University for two years, but dropped out after becoming more interested in art and performance. Humphries was particularly drawn to the absurdist art movement known as Dadaism.

DAME EDNA EVERAGE AND SIR LES PATTERSON

After leaving university, Humphries joined the newly created Melbourne Theatre Company and first brought to life the prototype of his best known character, an ordinary housewife from Moonee Ponds named Edna Everage, who later morphed into the international megastar Dame Edna Everage. Known for her bejewelled glasses, Edna always greets audiences with the words, 'Hello, possums!' Humphries' other famous characters include the 'cultural attaché' Sir Les Patterson who, through his use of Australian slang (much of which Humphries invented), his drunken antics and lewd actions, makes Australian culture seem ridiculous. These characters, especially Dame Edna Everage, helped make Humphries famous and have appeared in his stage and television shows, as well as in films.

Humphries first moved to the UK in 1959 and has lived there for most of his working life, although he returns to Australia regularly. In 2012 he announced he was retiring from show business and embarked on an Australian farewell tour called 'Eat, Pray, Laugh!'

NOTABLE HONOURS & AWARDS

Officer of the Order of Australia (1982)

Centenary Medal (2001)

Commander of the Order of the British Empire (2007)

Peter Allen
(1944–1992)

KEY ACHIEVEMENT
Wrote and performed the iconic song 'I Still Call Australia Home'

EARLY YEARS

Performer Peter Allen was born in Tenterfield, New South Wales. He began taking singing and dancing lessons when he was six years old. By the time he was 11, Allen was playing piano part-time at a local pub in Armidale.

INTERNATIONAL SUCCESS AND 'I STILL CALL AUSTRALIA HOME'

In 1959, Allen moved to Surfers Paradise, where he formed a popular cabaret and TV act called The Allen Brothers with his friend Chris Bell. The Brothers gained a following when they appeared on *Bandstand*, a popular television music show at that time.

In 1962 Allen and Bell set off on a tour of Asia. Two years later, they were spotted by famous American singer and actress Judy Garland, who invited them to be the opening act for her American concert tour. The Allen Brothers had a successful cabaret career in America until 1970, when they decided to separate.

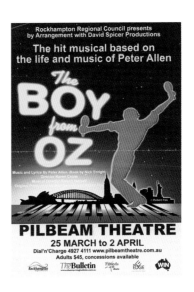

Rockhampton Regional Council presents by Arrangement with David Spicer Productions

The hit musical based on the life and music of Peter Allen

The BOY from OZ

Music and Lyrics by Peter Allen, Book by Nick Enright

PILBEAM THEATRE
25 MARCH to 2 APRIL
Dial'n'Charge 4927 4111 www.pilbeamtheatre.com.au
Adults $45, concessions available

Allen started writing and recording his own songs in 1971, as well as writing songs for other musicians. In 1979 his one-man show 'Up in One' opened on Broadway and he toured the show to Australia in 1980. It was during this tour that Allen wrote the now iconic song 'I Still Call Australia Home'.

Allen released his most successful album, *Bi-Coastal,* in 1980. And in 1982 he received an Academy Award for his contribution to the song 'Arthur's Theme (The Best That You Can Do)' from the movie *Arthur.*

Six years after Allen's death in 1992, a stage musical based on his life called *The Boy from Oz* opened in Australia. The show was so popular it became the first-ever Australian musical to be performed on Broadway in New York.

Clive James

BORN▪1939

Writer and critic Clive James is known for his humorous television chat shows, social commentary and ongoing series of autobiographies beginning with *Unreliable Memoirs* in 1980. James was appointed Commander of the Order of the British Empire in 2012 for services to literature and the media, and made an Officer of the Order of Australia in 2013.

The Wiggles

ESTABLISHED▪1991

One of Australia's most popular children's entertainment groups, The Wiggles have achieved widespread success both here and overseas. They have received numerous awards in Australia and America. In 2011 The Wiggles were inducted into the ARIA (Australian Recording Industry Association) Hall of Fame.

Steve Irwin

BORN▪1962   DIED▪2006

Steve Irwin was a wildlife expert known for his documentary TV series *The Crocodile Hunter*, which promoted the conservation of reptiles and animals. Irwin inherited his parents' reptile and fauna park in Queensland, renaming it Australia Zoo in 1992. The zoo continues to be one of Australia's most popular tourist destinations. Irwin was considered one of the country's top exports, receiving the Centenary Medal for his service to global conservation and to Australian tourism in 2001.

Slim Dusty
(1927–2003)

KEY ACHIEVEMENT
First Australian to have a number one hit song and a gold platinum album

EARLY YEARS

Country music singer Slim Dusty was born at Nulla Nulla Creek, New South Wales. He was born as David Gordon Kirkpatrick, but adopted the stage name 'Slim Dusty' when he left school at the age of 12 to pursue a career in country music. Dusty taught himself to play guitar by listening to the radio and copying his favourite musicians.

COUNTRY MUSIC

Dusty got his first recording contract in 1946, when he was 19 years old, following the success of his song 'The Rain Tumbles Down in July', which he had written and recorded the previous year. It was one of the first country songs about the Australian bush, and many people credit it as the start of Australian country music.

In 1951 Dusty married Jo McKean, who became his manager. Together, they toured around Australia as part of the Slim Dusty Travelling Show.

In 1957 'A Pub With No Beer', a song Dusty adapted from a poem by Gordon Parsons, became the first Australian single to go gold and was the biggest-selling record by an Australian at that time. Two years later Dusty wrote and recorded a sequel, 'The Answer To A Pub With No Beer'.

Dusty's successful career lasted nearly seven decades. He received an unmatched 37 Golden Guitar trophies from the Country Music Awards of Australia and two ARIA Music Awards, and was inducted into the ARIA Hall of Fame and the Country Music Roll of Renown. When he died at 76, Dusty had been working on his 106th album and had sold more than seven million records in Australia alone.

NOTABLE HONOURS & AWARDS

Member of the Order of the British Empire (1970)

Officer of the Order of Australia (1998)

Jimmy Little

BORN ▪ 1937   DIED ▪ 2012

Indigenous musician Jimmy Little made a huge contribution to Australian musical life, and was also an ambassador for Aboriginal culture. One of Little's most popular songs was the gospel tune 'Royal Telephone,' which was released in 1963. He was inducted into the ARIA Hall of Fame and won an ARIA Award for Best Adult Contemporary Album in 1999. Little was appointed an Officer of the Order of Australia in 2004 and was named a National Living Treasure the same year.

M. Yunupingu

BORN ▪ 1956   DIED ▪ 2013

Indigenous musician M. Yunupingu came to public attention as the front man of the band Yothu Yindi, whose number one song 'Treaty' in 1991 served as a political statement to the government of that time. Yunupingu was named Australian of the Year in 1993.

Doc Neeson

BORN ▪ 1947

Lead singer of the iconic Australian rock band The Angels. Doc Neeson was awarded an Order of Australia Medal in 2013 for his services to the performing arts.

Olivia Newton-John

BORN ▪ 1948

Singer, songwriter and actress Olivia Newton-John is most famous for her role as Sandy in the film *Grease* (1978), alongside John Travolta. Her records have sold over 100 million copies worldwide and she has won four Grammy Awards for her music. Newton-John was made an Officer of the British Empire in 1979 and an Officer of the Order of Australia in 2006.

John Farnham

BORN ▪ 1949

John Farnham is one of the country's best known performers, whose album *Whispering Jack* is the highest-selling album in Australian history. Farnham is the only Australian to have a number one record in five consecutive decades, and has received 19 ARIA awards throughout his career. He was named the 1987 Australian of the Year, appointed an Officer of the Order of Australia in 1996 and inducted into the ARIA Hall of Fame in 2003.

Jimmy Barnes

BORN ▪ 1956

Singer and songwriter for Cold Chisel, Jimmy Barnes is one of Australia's most successful musical groups. Barnes has had 14 Australian Top 40 albums with Cold Chisel and 13 solo albums, with nine of these solo albums reaching the number one position. He was inducted into the ARIA Hall of Fame in 2005.

Nick Cave

BORN ▪ 1957

Musician, composer, writer and actor Nick Cave is best known as the lead singer of the band Nick Cave and the Bad Seeds. The Bad Seeds formed in 1983 and have had great success in Australia and overseas. Cave was inducted into the ARIA Hall of Fame in 2007 and has won many national and international music awards.

Michael Hutchence

BORN ▪ 1960   DIED ▪ 1997

Michael Hutchence was the founding member, lead singer and songwriter of the internationally famous rock band INXS. Hutchence won Best International Artist and INXS won the group award at the 1991 Brit Awards (British equivalent of the Grammy Awards) celebrating popular music. He also played the lead role in the Australian cult film *Dogs in Space* (1986).

Kylie Minogue

BORN ▪ 1968

Singer and actress Kylie Minogue is one of Australia's most successful musical exports. Some of her popular songs include 'The Loco-Motion' (1987), which was the highest-selling Australian single of the 1980s, 'I Should Be So Lucky' (1988), 'Spinning Around' (2000) and 'Can't Get You Out of My Head' (2001). Minogue has received many music awards, including a number of ARIA and Brit Awards and a Grammy Award. She was appointed an Order of the British Empire in 2008 for services to music and was inducted into the ARIA Hall of Fame in 2011.

Archie Roach

BORN ▪ 1956

Musician, singer and songwriter Archie Roach is considered to be one of the most important Indigenous voices in Australia. His song 'Took the Children Away', about Australia's Stolen Generation, won two ARIA Awards and a Human Rights Achievement Award. In 2011 Roach was awarded the prestigious Red Ochre Award for his contribution to Aboriginal and Torres Strait Islander arts. He was also a state finalist for Australian of the Year in 2011.

❝ I'm very happy to hear that my work inspires writers and painters. It's the most beautiful compliment, the greatest reward. Art should always be an exchange. ❞

– Nick Cave

❝ I'm lucky that I have music and am able to get it out through songs. Some people don't have that luxury. ❞

– Archie Roach

Award-winning director **GEORGE MILLER** studied medicine at university with his twin brother, while at the same time making short films with one of his younger brothers.

Peter Finch was the first Australian to win a Best Actor Academy Award posthumously (after his death). Heath Ledger was the second Australian to do so.

Well loved singer **GLADYS MONCRIEFF** was known as 'Australia's Queen of Song' in the 1900s, performing in the opera *The Maid of the Mountains* – the most frequently revived musical of the Australian stage during that period.

Lead singer of Yothu Yindi, **M. YUNIPINGU**, was the first Indigenous person from Arnhem Land to receive a university degree, and by 1990 he was the first Aboriginal school principal in Australia.

WHEN THEATRE DIRECTOR JIM SHARMAN WAS YOUNG, HE SPENT TIME TRAVELLING WITH THE **CIRCUS**, AS HIS FATHER AND GRANDFATHER TOOK THEIR SIDESHOW BOXING ACT FROM SHOWGROUND TO SHOWGROUND.

Before becoming a pop singer, **Kylie Minogue** started out on the TV soap opera *Neighbours*.

Actor **RUSSELL CROWE** is a huge supporter of the national rugby league club the Sydney Rabbitohs. He was once a proud co-owner of the club.

GOLD LOGIE AWARD* WINNERS

1960	Graham Kennedy
1961	Bob Dyer
1962	Lorrae Desmond and Tommy Hanlon Jr
1963	Michael Charlton
1964	Bobby Limb
1965	Jimmy Hannan
1966	Gordon Chater
1967	Graham Kennedy and Hazel Phillips
1968	Brian Henderson
1969	Graham Kennedy
1970	Barry Crocker and Maggie Tabberer
1971	Gerard Kennedy and Maggie Tabberer
1972	Gerard Kennedy
1973	Tony Barber
1974	Graham Kennedy and Pat McDonald
1975	Ernie Sigley and Denise Drysdale
1976	Norman Gunston and Denise Drysdale
1977	Don Lane and Jeanne Little
1978	Graham Kennedy
1979	Bert Newton
1980	Mike Walsh
1981	Bert Newton
1982	Bert Newton
1983	Daryl Somers
1984	Bert Newton
1985	Rowena Wallace
1986	Daryl Somers
1987	Ray Martin
1988	Kylie Minogue
1989	Daryl Somers
1990	Craig McLachlan
1991	Steve Vizard
1992	Jana Wendt
1993	Ray Martin
1994	Ray Martin
1995	Ray Martin
1996	Ray Martin
1997	Lisa McCune
1998	Lisa McCune
1999	Lisa McCune
2000	Lisa McCune
2001	Georgie Parker
2002	Georgie Parker
2003	Rove McManus
2004	Rove McManus
2005	Rove McManus
2006	John Wood
2007	Kate Ritchie
2008	Kate Richie
2009	Rebecca Gibney
2010	Ray Meagher
2011	Karl Stefanovic
2012	Hamish Blake
2013	Asher Keddie

* The Gold Logie Award is presented to the most popular personality on Australian television, and is voted by the Australian public.

While on holiday in Egypt when she was 18, actress **Cate Blanchett** was invited to be an extra in a crowd scene of a local movie.

Nellie Stewart is considered to be Australia's greatest singing actress of the 19th century. She is best known for her role in the 1911 silent film SWEET NELL OF OLD DRURY.

Social commentator **CLIVE JAMES'** birth name was 'Vivian', but he soon changed this to 'Clive' because everyone thought 'Vivian' was a girl's name.

"The finest of athletes have, along with skill, a few more essential qualities: to conduct their life with dignity, with integrity, with courage and modesty. All these, are totally compatible with pride, ambition, determination and competitiveness."

– Donald Bradman

SPORT

ZOOM LENS
1:3.5-5.6
MADE IN WORLD
Fitzroy
Grange
GREAT
AUSTRAL
Laverton
VICTORIA DESE
Nullarbor Plain
Penong
GREAT
AUSTRALIAN BIGHT
Torrens
Woomera
Port Au
Pt. Pi
Kan-
garoo
Gambi

Victor Trumper

BORN ▪ 1877   DIED ▪ 1915

Cricketer Victor Trumper was considered by many as the most exciting batsman of the Golden Age of Cricket, before the devastation of the First World War. In his greatest innings, Trumper became the first player to make a century on the first morning of a Test match. He was also integral to the foundation of rugby league in Australia, and was the first treasurer of the NSW Rugby Football League. Trumper was named as *Wisden's* (a Cricketer's Almanac) Cricketer of the Year in 1903. He was inducted into the Australian Cricket Hall of Fame in 1996.

Roy Cazaly

BORN ▪ 1893   DIED ▪ 1963

Australian Rules football player Roy Cazaly was famous for his high marks (the clean catch of a kicked ball that has travelled more than 15 metres without being touched or hitting the ground), which inspired the catchphrase 'Up There, Cazaly' that is still used today. He was awarded Legend status by the Australian Football Hall of Fame in 1996.

Hubert Opperman

BORN ▪ 1904   DIED ▪ 1996

Former champion cyclist and politician Hubert Opperman remains the only Australian to have been voted European Sportsman of the Year, and who, as a politician, helped bring an end to the White Australia Policy. Opperman was appointed an Officer of the Order of the British Empire in 1953, a Knight Bachelor in 1968 and awarded the Gold Medal of the City of Paris in 1991.

Donald Bradman
(1908–2001)

KEY ACHIEVEMENT
Australia's greatest
Test batsman

EARLY YEARS

Cricketer Donald Bradman was born in Cootamundra, New South Wales, but his family moved to Bowral when he was two. He played cricket from a young age and practised batting constantly. Bradman hit his first century at the age of 12 as part of his school team. After leaving school at the age of 14, he continued to play cricket for his local Bowral side.

TEST CRICKET

Bradman was a standout player for his local cricket team in the district competition and his talent was soon noticed by the New South Wales Cricket Association, who invited him to the Sydney Cricket Ground for a practice session. In 1926 Bradman was selected to play grade cricket for St George in Sydney. The following season, at the age of 19, he was selected for the first-class New South Wales team.

Bradman made his Test debut in the 1928–29 Ashes series and went on to dominate international cricket during the 1930s. He represented Australia in 52 Test matches, scoring a total of 6,996 runs, with a batting average of 99.94. This was almost double that of his nearest rivals. Throughout his career, Bradman broke records for both first class and Test cricket. His highest international score of 334 remained unbeaten for decades as the highest ever international score by an Australian.

NOTABLE HONOURS & AWARDS

Knight Bachelor (1949)

Companion of the Order of Australia (1976)

One of *Wisden's* Five Cricketers of the 20th Century (2000)

International Cricket Council Hall of Fame (2009)

Jack Brabham

BORN • 1926

Australia's most successful racing car driver Jack Brabham was Formula One World Champion three times in 1959, 1960 and 1966. Brabham was appointed Officer of the Order of the British Empire and Australian of the Year in 1966, a Knight Bachelor in 1978, and an Officer of the Order of Australia in 2008. He won an Australian Sports Medal in 2000 and a Centenary Medal the following year. In 2012 Brabham was named a National Living Treasure.

Phar Lap

BORN • 1926   DIED • 1932

Phar Lap was a champion racehorse who has become a national legend. Phar Lap dominated the national and international racing scene in the late 1920s, before dying suddenly of an unknown illness. He was only five years old.

John Landy

BORN • 1930

John Landy is a former athletics champion best known for his achievement at an international meet in 1954, when he became the second man to break the four-minute mile in the one mile event. Landy was Governor of Victoria from 2001 to 2006. Landy is a Member of the Order of the British Empire, a Companion of the Order of Australia, and a Commander of the Royal Victorian Order.

Bart Cummings
(1927–)

KEY ACHIEVEMENT
Trained a record number of Melbourne Cup-winning horses

EARLY YEARS

Horse trainer Bart Cummings was born in Adelaide, South Australia. After finishing high school, Cummings started working with his father, who was also a champion horse trainer. Bart got his own training licence in 1953.

TRAINING CAREER

In 1958, Cummings won his first major race, the South Australian Jockey Club Derby, with a horse called Stormy Passage. He has gone on to train stakes winners every year since then.

The 1965–1966 racing season was a big one for Cummings. He won his first Trainer's Premiership, claimed his first Melbourne Cup victory, and won the Adelaide, Caulfield, Sandown, Sydney, Brisbane and Queen's cups.

In 2008 Cummings won the Melbourne Cup with an Australian thoroughbred named Viewed. It was his 12th Melbourne Cup victory and was also the 50th anniversary of the day he entered his first Melbourne Cup runner.

NOTABLE HONOURS & AWARDS

Member of the Order of Australia (1982)

Sport Australia Hall of Fame (1991)

Australian Racing Hall of Fame (2001)

> **"** I still love what I do and I've done okay over the years . . . You're a long time retired and anyway, I'd get bored.**"**
>
> – Bart Cummings

> **"From our broadcasting box you can't see any grass at all. It is simply a carpet of humanity."**
>
> *– Richie Benaud*

Richie Benaud

BORN ▪ 1930

Richie Benaud is a former cricket great, celebrated test captain and sports commentator. Benaud's unique style of commentary since he retired in 1964 has entertained and educated millions of cricket fans around the world. Benaud was made an Officer of the Order of the British Empire in 1961 for services to cricket. In 2007 he was inducted into the Australian Cricket Hall of Fame, and in 2009 he was inducted into the International Cricket Council Cricket Hall of Fame.

Ron Barassi

BORN ▪ 1936

Former Australian Rules football player and coach, who was the first player to be inaugurated into the Australian Football Hall of Fame as a Legend. He played 204 games for Melbourne between 1953 and 1964 and 50 games for Carlton between 1965 and 1969, scoring 330 goals in total. Barassi also had a successful coaching career and many consider his technique and rapport with his players to have been revolutionary. He coached Carlton from 1965 to 1971, North Melbourne from 1973 to 1980, Melbourne in 1964 and then from 1981 to 1985, and the Sydney Swans from 1993 to 1995 – making a total of 515 games with four premiership wins.

Dawn Fraser
(1937–)

KEY ACHIEVEMENT
Won gold in the same Olympic event three times in a row

EARLY YEARS

Champion Olympic swimmer Dawn Fraser was born in Balmain, New South Wales. She first started swimming at her local pool in an attempt to combat the asthma from which she suffered. In 1952, when she was 15 years old, her talent was noticed by coach Harry Gallagher, who took over Fraser's training. In 1955 Fraser won her first national title in the 220 yards (201 metres) freestyle. In the same year, she went on to set new records in all national freestyle events.

OLYMPICS

In 1956 Fraser became a national hero at the Melbourne Olympics when she broke the world record and won gold in the 100 metres freestyle. She also won gold in the 100 metres freestyle relay and silver in the 400 metres freestyle.

Fraser again took out the gold medal in the 100 metres freestyle at both the 1960 and 1964 Olympics, making her the first swimmer to win gold for the same event in three consecutive Olympic Games.

In her 15-year swimming career, Fraser broke 41 world records and won eight Olympic medals – four gold and four silver – as well as six Commonwealth Games medals and many Australian Championship medals. Fraser stopped swimming professionally after the 1964 Olympics.

NOTABLE HONOURS & AWARDS

Australian of the Year (1964)

Member of the Order of the British Empire (1967)

Officer of the Order of Australia (1998)

Australia's Greatest Female Athlete in History (1998)

Australian Hall of Fame Female Athlete of the Century (1999)

International Olympic Committee – World's Greatest Living Female Water Sports Champion (1999)

Australia's Greatest Female Athlete (2013)

❝ It's a beautiful thing, diving into the cool crisp water and then just sort of being able to pull your body through the water and the water opening up for you. ❞

– Dawn Fraser

Ron Clarke

BORN · 1937

One of the world's best known distance runners in the 1960s, Ron Clarke won four silver medals at the Commonwealth Games between 1962 and 1970 and a bronze medal at the Tokyo Olympics in 1964. He set 17 world records throughout his career. In 2013 he was appointed an Officer of the Order of Australia.

Betty Cuthbert

BORN · 1938

Champion sprinter in the 1950s and 1960s Betty Cuthbert broke 12 world records, and won four Olympic gold medals and one Commonwealth gold. She is the only Australian athlete to have won gold medals in the 100-metre, 200-metre and 400-metre Olympic sprinting events. Cuthbert was appointed a Member of both the Order of Australia and the Order of the British Empire, and is a National Living Treasure.

Herb Elliott

BORN · 1938

Accomplished middle-distance runner Herb Elliott won two gold medals at the 1958 Commonwealth Games. He also won gold in the 1960 Olympic Games, when he set a new world record in the 1500-metre run. He was appointed a Member of the Order of the British Empire in 1964, and a Companion of the Order of Australia in 2002. Elliott is a National Living Treasure.

Rod Laver

BORN ▪ 1938

Former champion tennis player Rod Laver holds the record for most singles titles won in the history of tennis. He is the only tennis player to have won the Grand Slam (all four major singles titles in the same year) twice. Throughout his career, Laver won 19 major tournaments, including 11 Grand Slam tournament titles. He won on all the tennis court surfaces (grass, clay and wood/parquet) used when he was playing. Laver was appointed a Member of the Order of the British Empire in 1970, and inducted into the International Tennis Hall of Fame in 1981. He was awarded the Australian Sports Medal in 2000 and is an Australian Living Treasure.

Johnny Warren

BORN ▪ 1943   DIED ▪ 2004

Former champion soccer player, coach and ambassador for soccer in Australia, Johnny Warren played 42 international matches in total, including Australia's first World Cup appearance in 1974. After he retired from playing, Warren campaigned to raise the profile of soccer in Australia. The award for the best player in the A-League is named the Johnny Warren Medal in his honour. In 1974 Warren was appointed a Member of the Order of the British Empire. In 1988 he was inducted into the Sport Australia Hall of Fame. He was awarded a Member of the Order of Australia in 2002. A year later he received the Fédération International de Football Association (FIFA) Centennial Order of Merit for his services to the game of soccer in Australia.

John Newcombe

BORN ▪ 1944

Former tennis player John Newcombe won 26 grand slam titles in singles, doubles, and mixed doubles over the course of his career. Newcombe has been named the Officer of the Order of Australia and an Order of the British Empire. He was inducted into the International Tennis Hall of Fame in 1986.

Peter Brock

BORN ▪ 1945 DIED ▪ 2006

One of the most successful motor racing drivers in Australian history. Brock won the Bathurst 1000 endurance race nine times, the Sandown 500 touring car race nine times, the Australian Touring Car Championship three times and the Bathurst 24 Hour once. He was made a Member of the Order of Australia in 1980 for service to the sport of motor racing. He received the Australian Sports Medal in 2000, the Centenary Medal in 2001, and the National Service Medal in 2006 for his military service between 1965–1967. Brock was inducted into the V8 Supercar Hall of Fame in 2001.

Lionel Rose

BORN ▪ 1948 DIED ▪ 2011

One of Australia's most successful boxers, Rose competed in the Bantamweight category (weighing between 52.163 and 53.525 kg), winning a total of 42 out of 53 fights in his career. He was named Australian of the Year in 1968 – the first Indigenous Australian to receive this honour – and made a Member of the Order of the British Empire that same year. In 2003 Rose was inducted into the Australian National Boxing Hall of Fame.

❝When you have a dream, you have to work hard to achieve that dream. Your dreams when you are young can be the force that keeps you going.❞

– Evonne Goolagong Cawley

Evonne Goolagong Cawley (1951–)

KEY ACHIEVEMENT
World number one
female tennis player

EARLY YEARS

Tennis champion Evonne Goolagong Cawley was born in Griffith, New South Wales and grew up in the small country town of Barellan. When she was five, Goolagong Cawley earned pocket money by retrieving balls at Barellan War Memorial Tennis Club. She got her first tennis racquet at the age of six and was encouraged to play at the local courts. In 1967, at the age of 16, her talent was spotted by top Sydney coach Vic Edwards, who persuaded Goolagong Cawley's parents to let her move to Sydney to train with him.

WORLD NUMBER ONE

After two years training with Edwards in Sydney, Goolagong Cawley made her Wimbledon debut at the age of 18 in 1970. The following year she won the women's singles titles at both the French Open and Wimbledon, becoming an instant celebrity in Australia and around the world.

Goolagong Cawley was ranked in the top ten international tennis players throughout the 1970s, reaching world no. 1 for a week in 1976. Throughout her career she won seven Grand Slam singles titles from 18 finals, and 13 major titles in total. In 1980 Goolagong Cawley won Wimbledon as a mother, only the second woman to have done so. The only major title she didn't win was the US Open.

NOTABLE HONOURS & AWARDS

Australian of the Year (1971)

Member of the Order of the British Empire (1972)

Officer of the Order of Australia (1982)

International Tennis Hall of Fame (1988)

Greg Norman

BORN ▪ 1955

Known as the 'Great White Shark', Greg Norman was a champion golf player who won more than 85 international tournaments throughout his career in the 1980s and 1990s. He has been made an Officer of the Order of Australia in recognition of his achievements.

Allan Border

BORN ▪ 1955

Former winning batsman and captain of the Australian cricket team, coach and television commentator Allan Border played 156 Test matches in his career and holds the world record for the greatest number of consecutive Test appearances, as well as the number of Tests as captain. In 1994 Border was named Queenslander of the Year and in 2009 he was one of the first 55 people inducted into the International Cricket Council Cricket Hall of Fame.

Shane Gould

BORN ▪ 1956

Former Olympic swimmer Shane Gould won three gold medals, one silver and one bronze at the 1972 Olympic Games. Gould holds the record of being the first female swimmer to win three Olympic gold medals in world-record time. She was appointed a Member of the Order of the British Empire in 1981, and was awarded the Australian Sports Medal in 2000 and the Centenary Medal in 2001 for her services to the sport of swimming in Australia.

Robert de Castella

BORN · 1957

Robert De Castella is a former world champion runner who holds the Oceanian Marathon record. His first big win was the 1981 Fukuoka Marathon in Japan. De Castella won a gold medal at the 1982 and 1986 Commonwealth Games, the 1983 World Athletic Championships and the 1986 Boston Marathon. In 1983 he was named Australian of the Year and received a Centenary Medal in 2001 for his achievements in marathon running. De Castella retired from the sport in 1993.

Pat Cash

BORN · 1965

Pat Cash is a former tennis champion and coach who won the 1987 Wimbledon Men's Singles title. In his playing career, Cash won six titles and was ranked world number four in 1988.

"There's a lot of heartache because you don't always win. You need lots of determination"

– Pat Cash

Cathy Freeman
(1973–)

EARLY YEARS

Former athletics champion Cathy Freeman was born in Mackay, Queensland. She won her first medal for running at a school athletics championship when she was eight years old. Freeman trained with her stepfather, Bruce Barber, an athletics coach, until she was 16. In 1987 she won a scholarship to a boarding school in Toowoomba, but moved to the Kooralbyn International School so she could train professionally.

NOTABLE HONOURS & AWARDS

Australian of the Year (1998)

World Sportswoman of the Year (2001)

Medal of the Order of Australia (2001)

COMMONWEALTH AND OLYMPIC SUCCESS

In 1990 Freeman won gold as a member of the Australian 4 x 100 metre relay team at the Commonwealth Games. At the 1992 Barcelona Olympics, Freeman became the first Indigenous Australian to represent Australia in athletics. She won two gold medals at the 1994 Commonwealth Games and gold at two World Championships. At the 1996 Atlanta Olympics, Freeman faced a tough French opponent and, even though she came second, she achieved her personal best and ran the 400 metres in 48.63 seconds. Later that year, Freeman ran against her rival again in Europe and won. Many consider one of the highlights of her career to be the Sydney Olympics in 2000, when she finished the 400 metres in 49.13 seconds to take the gold. Freeman announced her retirement from athletics in 2003.

❝I was running since I was ten. Since grade one at school people looked at me and thought, oh gosh she can really run, she's a natural.❞

– Cathy Freeman

> **"Remember to do the things you enjoy, away from swimming, regularly."**
>
> – Ian Thorpe

Cadel Evans

BORN ▪ 1977

Cadel Evans is the only Australian to have won the Tour de France cycling tournament. Evans was made a Member of the Order of Australia in 2013 for significant service to cycling and the community.

Ian Thorpe

BORN ▪ 1982

Swimmer Ian Thorpe has won more Olympic medals than any other Australian athlete. In his career, Thorpe has broken 22 world records, won ten Commonwealth Games gold medals and 11 world championships. Nicknamed 'Thorpedo' for his speed, Thorpe has held the title of *Swimming World* Swimmer of the Year four times, and was the Australian Swimmer of the Year from 1999 to 2003. He was also named Young Australian of the Year in 2000 and was awarded the Medal of the Order of Australia in 2001.

Casey Stoner

BORN ▪ 1985

One of Australia's most successful motorcycle racers, Casey Stoner won two MotoGP championships before his retirement in 2012. He received an Order of Australia in 2013 for significant services to motorcycle racing.

Tennis player **Evonne Goolagong Cawley** is only the second mother to have won the Wimbledon title. She had a daughter in 1977 and won Wimbledon in 1980.

Allan Border's importance to the sport of cricket is recognised at an annual award ceremony when the Australian cricket player of the year receives the Allan Border Medal.

Marathon runner **Robert De Castella** was nicknamed '**Deek**' or '**Deeks**' and sometimes '**Tree**', because his thick strong legs are like tree trunks.

BOXER **LIONEL ROSE** STARTED A SINGING CAREER IN THE 1970S, RELEASING THE SINGLES 'I THANK YOU' AND 'PLEASE REMEMBER ME'.

In 2008 Racing NSW announced a new horseracing award called 'The Bart Cummings Medal' – named after the esteemed horseracing trainer.

EARLY IN HIS CAREER, CRICKETER AND SPORTS COMMENTATOR **RICHIE BENAUD** HIT A RECORD 100 RUNS IN 78 MINUTES – THE THIRD FASTEST TEST CENTURY OF ALL TIME AND THE SECOND FASTEST BY AN AUSTRALIAN PLAYER.

DONALD BRADMAN is the only Australian cricketer to have been knighted.

In 2000 the centre court at Melbourne Park, which today hosts the Australian Open, was named the **ROD LAVER** Arena in the tennis player's honour.

At 14, **IAN THORPE** was the youngest-ever male swimmer to represent Australia when he competed in the 1997 **Pan Pacific Championships** in Japan.

The iconic phrase 'Up there, Cazaly' – inspired by football player Roy Cazaly – was used as a battle cry by Australian forces during the Second World War.

"Never give up! People don't understand how persistent you have to be. You come up against an obstacle and you have to find a way of moving forward. You take detours, navigate between the obstacles and make it happen. Unless you are very strong and convinced you can succeed, you will be swept away."

– Frank Lowy

The Packer Family

Robert Clyde Packer

BORN = 1879   DIED = 1934

Journalist, editor and owner of former Australian newspapers *Smith's Weekly* and *The Daily Guardian*. Founder of the Packer media dynasty.

Frank Packer

BORN = 1906   DIED = 1974

Media owner who founded Australian Consolidated Press (ACP) and was the main stakeholder in the Nine television network. At the age of 17 Packer became a cadet journalist on his father's paper *The Daily Guardian*. By the time he was 21 he was director of his father's company.

In 1933 Packer launched *The Australian Women's Weekly*. In 1934 he inherited his father's media interests, and two years later he formed ACP. He remained chairman of the company until 1974. In 1956 Packer branched out into television and had a significant holding in Nine Network Australia. He was knighted in 1959 for his services to journalism and was appointed a Knight Commander of the Order of the British Empire in 1971.

Kerry Packer

BORN = 1937   DIED = 2005

Media tycoon who owned Publishing and Broadcasting Limited (PBL). Packer inherited the ACP media company from his father, Frank Packer. In 1994 Kerry merged ACP with Nine Network Australia to form PBL. Packer also had interests in major national and international casinos, as well as in mining, pay television, land and tourism.

At the time of his death in 2005, Packer was the richest man in Australia. His son James Packer took over PBL after his death.

Kerry Packer was made a Companion of the Order of Australia in 1983.

The Murdoch Family

Keith Murdoch

BORN▪1885   DIED▪1952

Founding father of the Murdoch media empire. After a successful career as a journalist and influential newspaper editor, Murdoch became managing director, and later chairman, of the Herald Group, and from 1926 onwards began an aggressive campaign to take over newspapers around Australia. He made a move into newspaper ownership in 1948, when he acquired a minority interest in media company News Limited, which he left to his son Rupert when he died in 1952.

Rupert Murdoch

BORN▪1931

Founder and Executive Chairman of the global media group News Corp. In 1952 Murdoch inherited shares in the media company News Limited after the death of his father, Keith. Murdoch very quickly expanded his holdings by acquiring daily and suburban newspapers in almost every capital city in Australia. In 1964 he launched *The Australian*, the country's first national newspaper.

In 1979 Murdoch established News Corp and expanded his empire into the United States and London. Until June 2013, News Corp was a global multimedia company with interests in print, broadcast and new media. The company has now split into two separate divisions – 21st Century Fox, the entertainment arm, and News Corp, the publishing arm.

Murdoch was appointed a Companion of the Order of Australia in 1984.

> **❝ Money is not the motivating force.
> It's nice to have money, but I don't live high.
> What I enjoy is running the business. ❞**
>
> *– Rupert Murdoch*

John Darling

BORN ▪ 1831   DIED ▪ 1905

John Darling was founder of the flour milling and grain merchant company John Darling & Son. The company was established in 1872 and remained the largest miller in Australia for many years. Darling was known as 'Australia's Wheat King'.

Mei Quong Tart

BORN ▪ 1850   DIED ▪ 1903

Sydney tea merchant Mei Quong Tart was known for his large personality and diplomacy. When he was nine years old Quong Tart migrated to Australia from China with his family, who wanted to take advantage of the goldrush. In Australia Quong Tart was educated by a Scottish family and converted to Christianity. This education allowed him to act as a political representative for Chinese migrants, who were unpopular at the time. Quong Tart opened a number of successful tearooms in Sydney, serving tea imported from China.

Sidney Myer

BORN ▪ 1878   DIED ▪ 1934

Self-made businessman Sidney Myer founded the Myer department-store chain. Myer, who was born Simcha Baevski, immigrated to Australia from Russia in 1899. He opened his first shop in Melbourne in 1911. When Myer died, he left money in his will to establish the Sidney Myer Charitable Trust.

George Coles

BORN - 1885 DIED - 1977

Entrepreneur George Coles was one of the leading founders of G.J. Coles & Co in 1921. The company is now called the Coles Group and has become one of Australia's most successful supermarket franchises. Coles was made a Commander of the British Empire in 1942 and was knighted in 1957.

Reginald Ansett

BORN - 1909 DIED - 1981

Australian transport pioneer Reginald Ansett is best known as the founder of Ansett Transport Industries. Ansett Industries owned one of Australia's main domestic airlines between 1957 and 2001, as well as a number of road transport services. In the 1960s the business expanded into the TV industry with the purchase of ATV-0 in Melbourne. Ansett was knighted in 1969.

" You British reckon everything can be solved by compromise and diplomacy. We Australians fight to the very last ditch. "

– Kerry Packer

177

Lang Hancock

BORN ▪ 1909   DIED ▪ 1992

and

Gina Rinehart

BORN ▪ 1954

Lang Hancock was a mining magnate who built his fortune after discovering the world's largest iron ore deposit in the Hamersley Ranges in Western Australia in 1952. Hancock's daughter, Gina Rinehart, took over Hancock Prospecting after her father's death and has continued to expand the company. Rinehart is now Australia's richest person and the richest woman in the world.

Frank Lowy

BORN ▪ 1930

Businessman Frank Lowy co-founded the Westfield Group. The Group develops and builds shopping malls in Australia and around the world. Lowy is also known for donating generously to charity and for establishing a think tank called The Lowy Institute for International Policy. He has been made a Companion of the Order of Australia for his contribution to the Australian property and retail industries, as well as for his charity work.

"Beauty is an iron mine."

– Gina Rinehart

Robert Holmes à Court

BORN ▪ 1937   DIED ▪ 1990

Businessman Robert Holmes à Court is best known for being Australia's first billionaire.

Dick Smith

BORN ▪ 1944

Dick Smith is an entrepreneur, adventurer and environmental activist best known for developing the retail chain Dick Smith Electronics, as well as Dick Smith Foods. He was also instrumental in establishing *Australian Geographic* magazine. He was named Australian of the Year in 1986.

❝ If I could give a message to young Australians, it would be that success comes from being able to place yourself in a position where you have the freedom to do what you want to do. There is a greater chance of this happening in Australia than virtually any other country in the world . . . ❞

– Dick Smith

Entrepreneur Dick Smith is also a keen adventurer. He completed the first trans-Tasman balloon flight in 2000.

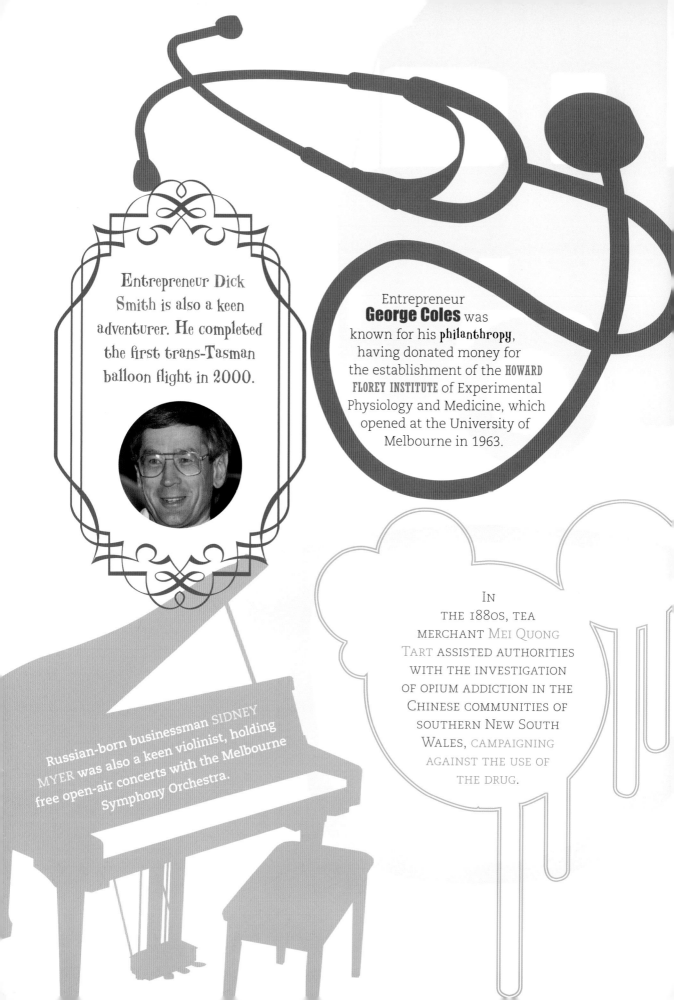

Entrepreneur **George Coles** was known for his philanthropy, having donated money for the establishment of the HOWARD FLOREY INSTITUTE of Experimental Physiology and Medicine, which opened at the University of Melbourne in 1963.

Russian-born businessman SIDNEY MYER was also a keen violinist, holding free open-air concerts with the Melbourne Symphony Orchestra.

IN THE 1880S, TEA MERCHANT MEI QUONG TART ASSISTED AUTHORITIES WITH THE INVESTIGATION OF OPIUM ADDICTION IN THE CHINESE COMMUNITIES OF SOUTHERN NEW SOUTH WALES, CAMPAIGNING AGAINST THE USE OF THE DRUG.

News Corp. Executive Chairman **RUPERT MURDOCH** has appeared as himself in episodes of *The Simpsons*.

Before founding Ansett Transport Industries, **REGINALD ANSETT** considered opening up a peanut farm, but thought against it after deeming it a potentially lonely life.

As well as being known for his business acumen, media tycoon **Kerry Packer** is also famous for founding World Series Cricket. It was staged between 1977 and 1979, and broadcast exclusively on the Nine Network.

Businessman and philanthropist FRANK LOWY was honoured in 1998 when Australia Post issued a postage stamp series on 'Australian Legends' that featured his face.

WHEAT MERCHANT **JOHN DARLING** WAS ONE OF THE FOUNDERS OF ADELAIDE OVAL. HE WAS INSPIRED BY HIS SON'S INTEREST IN THE CRICKET.

"My name is Edward Mabo, but my island name is Koiki. My family has occupied the land here for hundreds of years before Captain Cook was born. They are now trying to say I cannot own it."

– Edward Koiki Mabo

ZOOM LENS
1:3.5-5.6
18-80
SOCIAL JUSTICE
MADE IN WORLD
Fitzroy
Grange
GREAT
Bar
AUSTRA
VICTORIA DESE
Laverton
Nullarbor Plain
Penong
GREAT
AUSTRALIAN BIGHT
Woomera
L. Torrens
Port
Pt.
Kan-
garoo
Gamb

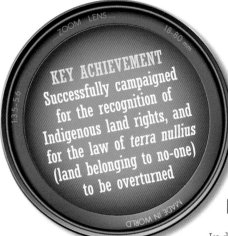

Edward Koiki Mabo
(1936–1992)

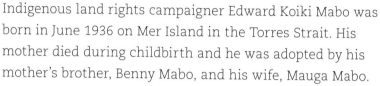

EARLY YEARS

Indigenous land rights campaigner Edward Koiki Mabo was born in June 1936 on Mer Island in the Torres Strait. His mother died during childbirth and he was adopted by his mother's brother, Benny Mabo, and his wife, Mauga Mabo.

Mabo was educated on Murray Island and moved to the Australian mainland when he was 21. He became involved in trade unionism while working on the Queensland railways and as a labourer for the Townsville Harbour Board. In 1962 Mabo became secretary of the Aboriginal Advancement League in Townsville, and in 1970 he was elected president of the Council for the Rights of Indigenous People.

1n 1967 Mabo became a gardener at James Cook University in Townsville. While working at the university, Mabo discovered that Murray Island was considered to be Crown land and was not owned by the Indigenous people who had always lived there. This was to be the start of his campaign for indigenous land rights.

NOTABLE HONOURS & AWARDS

Australian Human Rights Medal (1992)

CAMPAIGN FOR NATIVE TITLE

In 1981 a land rights conference was held at James Cook University and Mabo told the audience how the land inheritance system on Murray Island worked. The importance of Mabo's story was noted by a lawyer listening to his speech, who thought the current situation did not sound lawful and suggested they use the question of rightful ownership as a test case to claim land rights through the court system. The case raged back and forth in the courts for ten years until, finally, in 1992 the High court ruled that the Meriam people were entitled to the full ownership, occupation and use of Murray Island. This landmark decision incorporated the doctrine of native title into Australian law and rejected the idea that before European settlement Australia was *terra nullius* (land belonging to no one).

Mabo died in 1992. He was awarded the Australian Human Rights Medal in the Human Rights and Equal Opportunity Commission Awards later that year. The award (shared with other campaigners) recognised the long battle they fought to win justice for their people. James Cook University named its Townsville campus library the Edward Koiki Mabo Library in 2008. Mabo Day, celebrated on 3 June, is an official holiday in the Torres Shire.

Shirley Smith

BORN ▪ 1924   DIED ▪ 1998

Known as Mum Shirl, Shirley Smith was a prominent Aboriginal activist for Indigenous rights and welfare in Australia. Smith started her welfare work after her brother was imprisoned. She realised there were many prisoners who had no visitors and began to visit inmates in various prisons around New South Wales. It was during these visits that she came to be known affectionately as Mum Shirl. Smith was instrumental in establishing the Aboriginal Legal Service, the Aboriginal Medical Service, the Aboriginal Children's Service, the Aboriginal Tent Embassy and the Aboriginal Housing Company in Redfern, Sydney. Smith was made a Member of the Order of the British Empire in 1977 and of the Order of Australia in 1985. She was also a National Treasure.

> **"My grandfather said to me, 'You have to first love yourself, and spread it around'."**
>
> – *Shirley Smith*

Bob Maguire

BORN▪1934

Bob Maguire is a Roman Catholic priest and founder of the Father Bob Maguire Organisation, which offers practical help to disadvantaged members of society. Maguire is known for his creative and contemporary approach to social justice and has become a popular spokesperson on social justice issues in the Australian media. He was made a Member of the Order of Australia in 1989. In 2003 Maguire was named Entrepreneur of the Year for the Southern Region of Australia for a Social, Community or Not For Profit Organisation. He also received the Local Hero Victoria Award as part of the 2005 Australian of the Year celebrations.

Gabi Hollows

BORN▪1953

Gabi Hollows is founding director of The Fred Hollows Foundation, a non-profit organisation that works to prevent blindness and other eye diseases in Australia and overseas. The foundation was established in 1992 by Gabi's husband, the opthalmologist Fred Hollows, shortly before he died. Gabi worked with Fred to promote eye health in poor communities and has continued to do so, through the foundation, since his death. In 2001 she was awarded the Centenary Medal for services to community welfare and development. Hollows was made an Officer of the Order of Australia in 2013 and has been named a National Living Treasure.

> **"A smile is just such an amazing thing. And to think that some of those people can now smile because they can see you, that gives me that sort of charge, energy . . . that's what powers up my batteries. That's the joy that I have and that keeps me going. That's my rocket fuel, I suppose."**
>
> *– Gabi Hollows*

Chris Riley

BORN ▪ 1954

Roman Catholic priest Chris Riley has worked with disadvantaged teenagers for more than 35 years. He is founder and chief executive officer (CEO) of Youth Off the Streets, a non-denominational community organisation for young people who are homeless, drug dependent or recovering from abuse. Riley was appointed a Member of the Order of Australia in 2006. In the same year he was also awarded the Human Rights Medal from the Human Rights and Equal Opportunity Commission. He was nominated for NSW Australian of the Year in 2012 for his work with disadvantaged youth.

Tim Costello

BORN ▪ 1955

Tim Costello is a Baptist minister, a campaigner for social democracy and the Chief Executive Officer (CEO) of World Vision Australia. Costello has been at the forefront of public debate on social justice issues such as homelessness, gambling, urban poverty and substance abuse, and has served on a number of social justice advisory boards. In 2004 he was named Victorian of the Year and was made an Officer of the Order of Australia in 2005. A year later he was named Victorian Australian of the Year.

Moira Kelly

BORN ▪ 1964

Moira Kelly is a humanitarian aid worker, both in Australia and overseas, and founder of the Children First Foundation, which brings medical treatment to children in disadvantaged communities around the world. Kelly became an Officer of the Order of Australia in 2001, and she was named Victorian of the Year in 2012. She has been nominated twice for Australian of the Year.

CEO of World Vision Australia **Tim Costello** is the brother of Peter Costello, the former Treasurer of Australia during the Howard Government era (1996–2007).

ABORIGINAL AND WELFARE ACTIVIST **Shirley Smith** IS THE ONLY WOMAN IN AUSTRALIA TO HAVE BEEN GRANTED ACCESS TO ALL PRISONS IN NEW SOUTH WALES.

IT IS SAID THAT HUMANITARIAN WORKER **GABI HOLLOWS** WAS INSPIRED TO LEARN MORE ABOUT MEDICINE AT THREE YEARS OLD WHEN SHE UNDERWENT EYE SURGERY.

Father Bob Maguire co-hosts the Triple J radio programme 'Sunday Night Safran' with documentary maker John Safran. They also appeared together on the SBS show *Speaking in Tongues*, which looked at topical issues with a religious perspective.

In 2009 Catholic priest **FATHER BOB MAGUIRE** wrote on his blog that he would resign from the priesthood on his 75th birthday, after being contacted by church authorities. However, he didn't retire until two years later, with his last church service **ATTENDED BY AROUND 1,000 PEOPLE**.

Founder of Children First Foundation, **MOIRA KELLY**, is the legal guardian of conjoined twins **Trishna** and **Krishna**, who were born in Bangladesh. The babies were separated in 2009 after a lengthy operation at Melbourne's Royal Children's Hospital. Kelly is also the adoptive mother of **Emmanuel** and **Ahmed Mustafa**, who were found in a shoe box in a park in Baghdad, Iraq.

IN A TITLE INDEPENDENT OF THE AUSTRALIAN OF THE YEAR AWARDS HELD BY THE AUSTRALIAN GOVERNMENT, INDIGENOUS LAND RIGHTS ACTIVIST EDWARD KOIKI MABO WAS APPOINTED AUSTRALIAN OF THE YEAR BY *THE AUSTRALIAN* NEWSPAPER IN 1993.

Before becoming a priest and CEO of Youth Off the Streets, **Father Chris Riley** worked as a **teacher**, **youth worker** and **probation officer**. He was also involved in the charity Boys' Town, and served as principal and residential care worker.

INDEX

REFERENCES

Atkinson, A., *The Dictionary of Famous Australians*, Allen & Unwin, 1992

Atkinson, A., Knight, L. & McPhee, M., *Dictionary of Performing Arts in Australia Volumes 1 & 2*, Allen & Unwin, 1996

Barnard, L., *30 Australian Sports Legends*, Random House Australia, 2008

Barnard, L., *Going for Gold: Australian Olympians and other Champions*, Random House Australia, 2012

Bebbington, W. A., *A Dictionary of Australian Music*, Oxford University Press, 1998

Brisbane, K., *Entertaining Australia*, Currency Press, 1991

Cheng, C. & Knight, L. in association with the Powerhouse Museum, *Australia's Greatest Inventions & Innovations*, Random House Australia, 2012

Collins, P., *Book People: Meet Australia's Children's Authors and Illustrators*, MacMillan Education Australia, 2002

Creswell, T. & Trenoweth, S., *100 Australians You Should Know*, Pluto Press, 2006

Davison, G., Hirst, J. & Macintyre, S. (eds), *The Oxford Companion to Australian History*, Oxford University Press, 2001

Ingram, A. & O'Donnell, P., *30 Australian Legends and Icons*, Random House Australia, 2006

Keneally, T., *Australians: Origins to Eureka*, Allen & Unwin, 2009

Keneally, T., *Australians: Eureka to The Diggers*, Allen & Unwin, 2011

McFarlane, I., *The Encyclopaedia of Australian Rock and Pop*, Allen & Unwin, 1999

Pan Macmillan Australia, *Macquarie Encyclopaedic Dictionary*, Pan Macmillan Australia, 2010

Random House Australia, *Australia Through Time 2009*, Random House Australia, 2009

Stanton, J. et al. (ed), *Australian Sport Through Time 2009*, Random House Australia, 2009

About Australia
www.australia.gov.au

Art Gallery of New South Wales
www.artgallery.nsw.gov.au

Australian Academy of Science
www.science.org.au

Australian Broadcasting Corporation – Famous Australians
www.abc.net.au/schoolstv/australians/austs.htm

Australian Dictionary of Biography
www.adb.anu.edu.au/

Australian War Memorial
www.awm.gov.au

Civics and Citizenship Education
www.civicsandcitizenship.edu.au

Migration Heritage, New South Wales
www.migrationheritage.nsw.gov.au

National Archives of Australia – Prime Ministers
www.primeministers.naa.gov.au

Study in Australia – Nobel Prize Winners
www.studyinaustralia.gov.au/en/Why-Study-in-Australia/
Nobel-Prize-Winners/Australian-Nobel-Prize-winners

Sydney Powerhouse Museum
www.powerhousemuseum.com

The Official Website of the Nobel Prize
www.nobelprize.org

Wikipedia
www.wikipedia.org

IMAGE CREDITS

PIONEERING AUSTRALIANS

p. 2 James Cook NAA: A1200/L56213; p. 3 Arthur Phillip NAA: A1200/L37363
p. 4 Joseph Banks NAA: A6135/K1/4/77/2; p. 5 John Macarthur: Mitchell Library, State Library of NSW – GPO1 – 06190; p. 6 Matthew Flinders NAA: A6180/30/1/74/17; p. 7 George Bass NAA: A1200/L24699; p. 8 Edward John Eyre NAA: A6135/K20/10/77/63; p. 9 Hamilton Hume: Mitchell Library, State Library of NSW – GPO1 – 18527; p. 9 Captain William Hilton Hovell: Mitchell Library, State Library of NSW – P1/780; p. 9 William Farrer NAA: C4078/N3188B; p. 10 Gregory Blaxland: Mitchell Library, State Library of NSW – GPO1 – 14069; p. 11 William Lawson: John Oxley Library, State Library of Queensland, Neg: 196536; p. 11 William Charles Wentworth NAA: A1200/L18585; p. 12 Henry Parkes NAA: A1200/L12687; p. 13 Robert O'Hara Burke: John Oxley Library, State Library of Queensland, Neg: 76942; p. 13 William John Wills NAA: A3560/6690; p. 14 Illustration of Mary MacKillop © Sonia Martinez 2013 from *Meet . . . Mary MacKillop* written by Sally Murphy and illustrated by Sonia Martinez, published by Random House Australia 2013; p. 16 Caroline Chisholm NAA: C4078/N17143; p. 17 portrait of Edith Cowan, National Library of Australia, an23351616; p. 18 Douglas Mawson NAA: B941/HISTORIC/ANTARCTIC/1; p. 21 Lawrence Hargrave NAA: A1200/L69328; p. 21 Bert Hinkler NAA: A1200/L36323; p. 22 Charles Kingsford Smith NAA: A1200/L96364; p. 24 portrait of Nancy Bird-Walton by Russell Roberts, National Library of Australia, an11333638

POLITICS

p. 30 Edmund Barton NAA: A5954/1299/2 PHOTO PL375/1; p. 31 Alfred Deakin NAA: AA1984/624/A2; p.32 William 'Billy' Hughes: W. M. Hughes, National Library of Australia, ms1538-10-339; p. 33 Robert Menzies NAA: A5954/1299/2 PHOTO L13044; p. 34 John Curtin NAA: A1200/11132323; p. 36 portrait of H. V. Evatt by Max Dupain, National Library of Australia, an25060678; p. 37 Harold Holt NAA: A1200/L49364; p. 38 Gough Whitlam NAA: A1200/L41571; p. 40 Neville Bonner NAA: A6180/17/5/76/24; p. 41 Malcolm Fraser NAA: A6180/6/1/78/2; p. 42 Donald Chipp NAA: A1501/A5188/1; p. 43 Bob Hawke © EdStock/iStockphoto; p. 44 Paul Keating NAA: A6180/10/11/95/1; p. 46 John Howard © EdStock/iStockphoto; p. 47 Julia Gillard © Bloomberg via Getty Images; p. 48 Prime Minister Kevin Rudd by Loui Seselja, National Library of Australia, nl40102-ls39

SCIENCE AND MEDICINE

p. 54 Howard Florey NAA: A1200/L1592; p. 55 Frank Macfarlane Burnet NAA: A1200; L36826; p. 56 portrait of Sir Edward Dunlop by John McKinnon, National Library of Australia, vn4584039; p. 58 portrait of Frank Fenner by Loui Seselja, National Library of Australia, an22966245; p. 59 Dorothy Hill NAA: A1200/L42648; p. 60 Vivian Bullwinkel NAA: A1501/A925/1; p. 61 portrait of Professor Fred Hollows, National Library of Australia, an22839744; p. 62 Professor Gustav Nossal by Reg Morrison, National Library of Australia, vn4994253; p. 64 Tim Flannery: Pictures Collection, State Library of Victoria, H2006.190/5; p. 66 Victor Chang © Steve Christo, Fairfax Images; p. 67 Charles Teo © Edwina Pickles, Fairfax Images; p. 68 Fiona Wood by Greg Power, National Library of Australia, nl39415-gp55

ARCHITECTURE AND DESIGN

p. 74 Francis Howard Greenway: Mitchell Library, State Library of NSW – GPO1 – 21951; p. 74 Edmund Thomas Blacket: Mitchell Library, State Library of NSW – GPO1 – 12251; p. 75 Parliament House in Canberra © FiledIMAGE/iStockphoto; p. 76 portrait of Dr John Bradfield by H. C. Krutli, National Library of Australia, an23278759; p. 77 Robin Boyd NAA: A1200/L53204;

p. 78 Australia Square © Breamy/iStockphoto; p. 80 Sydney Olympic railway station (Phillip Cox) © Kokkai/iStockphoto; p. 81 Australian outback hat (Akubra) © TarpMagnus/iStockphoto; p. 82 Florence Broadhurst NAA: A12111/1/1971/6/43; p. 83 Prue Acton NAA: A6135/K3/4/74/6; p. 84 RM Williams logo NAA: A6135/K26/7/88/72; p. 85 Jenny Kee NAA: A6135/1/85/23; p. 85 Colette Dinnigan © EdStock/iStockphoto; p. 85 Mambo image provided courtesy of Mambo Graphics; p. 86 Kuta Lines logo provided courtesy of Kuta Lines; p. 87 embryo chair by Marc Newson © Sheila Thomson 2007

FINE ARTS

p. 92 William 'Bill' Dobell by Hal Missingham, National Library of Australia, vn5978097; p. 93 *Shearing the Rams* by Tom Roberts NAA: A1200/L2328; p. 93 *Explorer Attacked by Parrots* by Albert Tucker NAA: A1200/L46979; p. 94 *Self-portrait* by Arthur Boyd NAA: A1200/L46968; p. 95 Albert Namatjira NAA: A1200/L7861; p. 96 Sidney Nolan NAA: A6180/11/3/75/7; p. 97 *The Drover's Wife* by Russell Drysdale NAA: A1200/ L36695; p. 101 Pro Hart by Michael Jensen, National Library of Australia, vn3550858; p. 101 Ken Done NAA: A6135/K11/9/92/10; p. 102 Frank Hurley, National Library of Australia, vn4915570; p. 102 Max Dupain © Jill White, National Library of Australia, an23235858; p. 103 Tracey Moffatt NAA: A6180/4/1/90/4; p. 104 Nellie Melba: John Oxley Library, State Library of Queensland, Neg: 40255; p. 105 Dame Joan Sutherland photographed by Don McMurdo, courtesy of Sydney Opera House Trust and National Library of Australia, an23382943; p. 106 Robert Helpmann, Apparitions by Gordon Anthony, National Library of Australia, an13030681; p. 107 Graeme Murphy by Branco Gaica, courtesy of Sydney Dance Company and National Library of Australia, an24914342; p. 108 portrait of Richard Tognetti by Greg Barrett, National Library of Australia, an11656063; p. 110 portrait of Kelvin Coe by Walter

Stringer, National Library of Australia, an24095825; p. 110 Lucette Aldous by John McKinnon, National Library of Australia, vn3305752; p. 111 Bernard Heinze NAA: A1200/L40102; p. 111 Charles Mackerras NAA: A1200/L36354

LITERATURE

p. 114 portrait of A. B. Paterson, National Library of Australia, an22199070; p. 115 Marcus Andrew Hislop Clarke: National Library of Australia, vn3663411; p. 115 Mary Gilmore NAA: A1200/L11410; p. 116 Henry Lawson: Mitchell Library, State Library of NSW – P1/952; p. 117 portrait of Henry Handel Richardson, National Library of Australia, an23436172; p. 118 Dorothea Mackellar: Mitchell Library, State Library of NSW – P1/1076; p. 119 cover of *The Complete Adventures of Snugglepot and Cuddlepie* by May Gibbs, published by HarperCollins Publishers Australia 2007; p. 121 Miles Franklin: Parker Studio, National Library of Australia, ms-ms681-0-2; p. 122 Patrick White NAA: A1200/L51614; p. 124 Christina Stead: National Library of Australia, an24717059; p. 125 Manning Clark NAA: A1501/A916/1; p. 126 Judith Wright NAA: A1200/L16977; p. 127 Robert Hughes © Rex Dupain, National Library of Australia, an14228829; p. 129 Peter Carey © Granville Davies; p. 130 portrait of Oodgeroo Noonuccal, National Library of Australia, an11618802

ENTERTAINMENT

p. 136 portrait of Louise Nelly Lovely, National Library of Australia, an12091515; p. 136 portrait of Judith Anderson by Florence Vandamm, National Library of Australia, an13180738; p. 136 portrait of Errol Flynn, National Library of Australia, an13384126; p. 137 Paul Hogan© EdStock/iStockphoto; p. 138 Russell Crowe© EdStock/iStockphoto; p. 138 Hugh Jackman© EdStock/iStockphoto; p. 140 Geoffrey Rush © EdStock/iStockphoto; p. 141 Peter Weir © EdStock/iStockphoto; p. 141 George Miller © EdStock/iStockphoto; p. 141 Phillip Noyce © EdStock/iStockphoto; p. 142 Mel Gibson ©

EdStock/iStockphoto; p. 143 Baz Luhrmann © EdStock/iStockphoto; p. 144 Dame Edna © Greg Gorman; p. 145 *The Boy from Oz* poster courtesy of Robert Fox, National Library of Australia, vn5970882; p. 147 portrait of Slim Dusty by Don McMurdo, National Library of Australia, an23356315; p. 148 portrait of Jimmy Little by Loui Seselja, National Library of Australia, an24523705; p. 148 M. Yunupingu © Jacqueline Mitelman, National Library of Australia, an14168947; p. 149 Olivia Newton-John © EdStock/iStockphoto; p. 149 Jimmy Barnes © EdStock/iStockphoto; p. 150 Nick Cave © EdStock/iStockphoto; p. 150 Kylie Minogue © EdStock/iStockphoto; p.152 portrait of Gladys Moncrieff, National Library of Australia, an23372005; p. 153 Nellie Stewart as 'Sweet Nell' NAA: A1861/17

SPORT

p. 156 Victor Trumper NAA: A1200/L46198; p. 156 Hubert Opperman NAA: A12111/1/1965/25/20; p.157 Don Bradman: Dixson Galleries, State Library of NSW – DG ON4/2356; p. 158 Jack Brabham NAA: B941/SPORT/MOTOR RACING/9; p. 158 Phar Lap NAA: J2879/QTH601/1; p. 158 John Landy NAA: A1200/L30013; p. 160 Ron Barassi: Mitchell Library, State Library of NSW – APA – 15030; p. 162 portrait of Betty Cuthbert, National Library of Australia, an23566804; p. 162 Herb Elliott, National Library of Australia, vn4584039; p. 164 Lionel Rose NAA: A1200/L71439; p. 165 Evonne Goolagong Cawley NAA: A6135/K27/1/72/17; p. 166 Greg Norman NAA: A6135/K3/3/87/14; p. 166 portrait of Shane Gould, National Library of Australia, vn3570195; p. 167 Robert de Castella by Wolfgang Sievers, National Library of Australia, vn3410575

p. 176 John Darling, State Library of South Australia – B 5622/25; p. 177 George Coles: courtesy of Collingwood Local History Photograph Collection; p. 177 portrait of Reginald Ansett, National Library of Australia, an22593026; p. 178 portrait of Frank Lowy by Gary Ede, National Library of Australia, an12483008; p. 179 photograph of Robert Holmes à Court sourced from the collections of the State Library of Western Australia, reproduced with the permission of the Library Board of Western Australia, no. 215795PD; p. 179 Dick Smith NAA: A6135/K23/5/91/1

SOCIAL JUSTICE

p. 184 Edward Koiki Mabo © News Ltd/Newspix